THE LARGER STEWARDSHIP

THE
LARGER STEWARDSHIP

By

CHARLES A. COOK

Author of "Stewardship and Missions,"
"God's Will and Our Life," etc.

———

PHILADELPHIA

THE JUDSON PRESS

| BOSTON | CHICAGO | LOS ANGELES |
| KANSAS CITY | SEATTLE | TORONTO |

Printed in U. S. A.

INTRODUCTION

In these times of stress for the world and for the church, it is a very hopeful sign that true Christians are beginning to take their religion more seriously. The proofs of this statement include not only a firmer determination to win the world for Christ, but a new emphasis on certain great doctrines of our religion, which have to do with the personal life and social influence of the Christian. These doctrines have always been believed, but have lain in the background of interest and thought. They now come to the front for greater emphasis, clearer definition, more specific application, and larger influence on the life of the church and the individual member of it. Such a doctrine is the motive power and *raison d'être* of the great and growing Stewardship Movement, which is now beginning to focus the attention of all denominations. That God is the Owner of all, and that we are stewards, or, in the more specific Christian form, " Ye are not your own; for ye were bought with a price " (1 Cor. 6 : 19, 20), even " with the precious blood of Christ " (1 Peter

1 : 19), is the central teaching of the Stewardship Movement, which this book unfolds with freshness and power.

In the earlier days of the new emphasis on stewardship, its relation to possessions received nearly exclusive attention. There was also a tendency at that time to an almost legalistic extreme, especially on the subject of tithing. Much excellent instruction along these lines was thereby compromised and rendered ineffective for certain minds. This book of Doctor Cook's gives us the larger and the better view. It still deals with the stewardship of property, but sees it as only one item in a far larger and more impressive whole. It therefore has an important mission, and we bespeak for it a wide reading and a prayerful consideration.

FREDERICK L. ANDERSON.

JANUARY 15, 1923.

FOREWORD

In the very general discussion of the subject of Christian Stewardship there has been a growing conviction that more attention needs to be given to the inner spiritual springs from which the streams of true stewardship living and practise flow. We must get back of the money question to the man himself, back of the collection to the character, back of what a man gives to what he is.

Many leaflets and pamphlets have briefly discussed certain phases of this deeper and more essential stewardship, but in no publication known to the writer have these various phases of the larger stewardship been fully considered and brought together in a single volume.

Belief that such a discussion might meet a real need and contribute toward a better understanding of the deep significance of the whole subject of Christian Stewardship, and help to a more effective and definitely spiritual application of the great principles involved, is the reason for this, another book on this almost inexhaustible theme.

Foreword

The very kind reception that has been given to his book " Stewardship and Missions " leads the author to indulge the hope that the present volume may be found worthy of interest and may contribute increased value to its predecessor.

Sincere acknowledgment of valuable suggestions by Dr. F. A. Agar, Church Efficiency Secretary of the Northern Baptist Convention, and by Dr. Joseph L. Peacock, President of Shaw University, is here made.

CHARLES A. COOK.

SEATTLE, WASH.

CONTENTS

CHAPTER I

THE LARGER STEWARDSHIP

1. Explanation

The stewardship that has to do with the administration of income and wealth, in the interests of the gospel of Jesus Christ, should be given the fullest consideration by Christians everywhere. Only a small proportion of church-members have, in loyalty to Jesus Christ, put their financial matters in getting, and giving, and using, on a stewardship basis for God and his world work. Notwithstanding all that has been done, and much has been done in these recent years, we have not much more than inaugurated the movement for a better stewardship of substance for the kingdom of God. There are vast resources of wealth in the possession of Christian men and women which have not yet been brought under the sanctifying power of the Holy Spirit, and that are not being administered along stewardship lines for Christ and the evangelization of the world. A more thorough and more general campaign to inculcate stewardship of this type needs to be vigorously prosecuted in all the churches. But important as this phase of stewardship is, and great as is the necessity for an earnest continuation of propaganda on its behalf among the churches, there is a stewardship that is greater and much more important.

This larger stewardship has to do with the life, the inner life, of the believer and with all the outer expression of that life. No man can be fully the kind of steward God wants him to be in relation to wealth until he learns the deeper lessons in the essentials of true stewardship living and service.

The stewardship which is discussed in these pages has to do primarily with spiritual values embodied in individuals, with the great realm occupied by the mind and heart, with the inherent things of life in their relation to God and to service in his kingdom. It has to do with what one is and does more than with what one has, though it does not lose sight of the substance which comes into our hand. It deals with the essential springs from which flow the most beneficent streams of living and service with which the church can be blessed, for life has constantly demonstrated that doing right comes in the long run from being habitually right with God. Greater power in the church, and larger service for Christ by the church, because of the richer faith and fuller consecration of individual Christians, must come through an apprehension and application of this larger stewardship.

Stewardship of money is only a fraction of our full Christian stewardship. Giving is only a fraction of our stewardship of money. Tithing is only a fraction of our stewardship in giving. All these have their place in the larger stewardship, but when put together they do not constitute full stewardship living, nor meet the boundless needs of the times. Nor does upright moral living meet the requirements of the larger stewardship without the consecration of the substance one holds to the service of God and humanity. The rich young ruler could say, " All these things have I kept from my youth up," but Jesus said to him, " One thing thou lackest." He was to give as well as live. A part is never equal to the whole. The call is for such stewardship living as will not be fractional, in which the whole life will be included, in which self and substance will both come under the rule of stewardship principles.

2. The Necessity

The conditions which prevail all too generally in the churches, and the urgent needs of the great world field with its myriads of open doors calling for workers, make necessary special emphasis on the larger stewardship. There are so many church-members of the Laodicean type who are

neither hot nor cold, who have a name to live
but are dead.   Says Doctor Jowett:

These Laodiceans were neutrals, devoid of passion, desti-
tute of any enthusiasm, loafing along in moral indifference.
In times of great crisis they were anyway, either way, altogether tepid regarding the issues.   And in times of great
laxity they maintained the same tepidity, utterly uncon-
cerned with the degeneracy.

The most the churches have of some members is
their names on the church roll.   That does not help
much.   Such members do not really *belong* to the
church.   People belong to the person or thing to
which they are most devoted; then how many
there are who have no right to say that they are
devoted to the church!   The church does not get
their service.   Their personal participation in the
services and activities of the church is nil.   They
are absentee members.   They are not functioning
as living parts of the great spiritual organism in
its divinely given mission in the world.   They
are like the tissue-paper flowers tied to the
branches of the Christmas tree, not a real part of
the tree in any vital sense.

Not every one that saith unto me, Lord, Lord, shall
enter into the kingdom of heaven; but he that doeth the
will of my Father who is in heaven (Matt. 7 : 21).

" The adhesion of the barnacle does not indicate
that it belongs to the vessel."   Clinging to the
church by having one's name on the church roll

does not prove that one belongs to the church. Proof is in living active participation in the worship and service of the church. Barnacles clinging to a ship do not help progress but hinder it. Mere nominal church-members hinder rather than help the church. It is genuine Christian living that is needed, and not simply having a name to live. Christian living involves the acknowledgment of the lordship of Jesus Christ in the life. When all the life is governed by that acknowledgment there will be what may properly be called stewardship living.

Discussion of this larger stewardship is necessary because so far what has been written has been limited, almost wholly, to the stewardship of property, the getting, and giving, and using of money. The more comprehensive subject has not been fully considered. Here and there the shores of this larger theme, the stewardship of all that is included in the life, have been touched, but the vast continent of truth, with all its boundless riches and highest spiritual values, has remained mostly unexplored. We have been very thoroughly taught concerning the stewardship of material things, and the church of Jesus Christ is a better church, and is doing better work in preaching the gospel of the grace of God to the nations, as a result of the lessons we have learned. The decided increase in Christian giving, the marked revival of tithing, the greater mobilization of the Christian forces of the world for the full carrying out of the great commission in these recent years, are all due, in no small measure, to the emphasis that has been placed on a Scriptural stewardship in the acquisition, giving, and use of money. But even when we have made the highest appraisement of all that this revival means we have still but a limited apprehension of the full significance of what is involved in stewardship living. We need to explore the important practical teachings to be found beyond the shore-line.

The larger stewardship needs to be inculcated in order to save the church from the clogging and deteriorating influences of its own unfaithful members. It needs to be taught to those who are about to enter the church in order that they may have a sense of their responsibility to God for the way they live from the very beginning of their regeneration and membership in the church. It needs to be taught in order that the church may no longer limp along with a fifty per cent. efficiency, or less, but may advance in power more nearly approximating an efficiency of one hundred per cent.

3. It Is Not Easy

This larger stewardship is not easy. It calls for the utmost of self and service. It is all-inclusive. No corner of one's life in any sphere or relationship is exempt from it. There is nothing we can be or do to which stewardship living does not apply. This is what makes it more difficult than the stewardship that is limited to a right administration of material things for Christ and his church. Its requirements are more complex. It is harder to live than it is to give. He who gives liberally may at the same time live unrighteously. Spiritual acts are more difficult than physical. It is easier to kneel than it is to pray. It is easier to send a check to the treasurer of the church, and pay one's subscription, than it is to take oneself and family to God's house and there sincerely worship God and have fellowship with his people. It is easier to unite with the church than it is to follow Christ as Lord. It is easier to give than to love. It is easier to profess than it is to possess and practise.

The larger stewardship calls for the higher and harder things. It is none too soon for the entire membership of the church to listen to such a call and to consider the real essentials of true Christian living from the stewardship standpoint. Great is the need for a revival of the New Testament conception of Christian discipleship and a return to the New Testament standard of church-membership. Too little has Christlike living and Christlike sacrificial service been lovingly and earnestly insisted upon as requisite to membership in the church. We have made it too easy to get into the church, and we have allowed it to be too easy to retain membership in good standing in the church. Where there is no sense of

B

personal responsibility for the support of the church, or for carrying on its mission in the world, church-membership does not mean much. They who have not taken up the cross involved in sincerely following Jesus Christ forfeit any claim to Christian discipleship. Jesus says so:

If any man cometh unto me, and hateth not his own father, and mother, and wife, and children, and brethren, and sisters, yea, and his own life also, *he cannot be my disciple.* Whosoever doth not bear his own cross, and come after me, *cannot be my disciple.* For which of you, desiring to build a tower, doth not first sit down and count the cost, whether he have wherewith to complete it? Lest haply, when he hath laid a foundation, and is not able to finish, all that behold begin to mock him, saying, This man began to build and was not able to finish. Or what king, as he goeth to encounter another king in war, will not sit down first and take counsel whether he is able with ten thousand to meet him that cometh against him with twenty thousand? Or else, while the other is yet a great way off, he sendeth an ambassage, and asketh conditions of peace. So therefore whosoever he be of you that renounceth not all that he hath, *he cannot be my disciple* (Luke 14 : 26-33).

The Lord Jesus did not make it easy for any one to become his follower. He insisted upon separation, surrender, sacrifice. No one of these requirements is easy; but when the believer, in loving loyalty to his Divine Leader, commits himself to them, and thereby enters the pathway of the larger stewardship, he finds a joy and blessedness never before discovered. He then comes into contact with the eternal sources of power, and his life is lifted away above the low, narrow, selfish, non-participating level on which so many abide. The harder thing becomes the unspeakably better thing because it is the really Christian thing.

4. Making Real the Ideals

Stewardship living calls for the making real in the lives of Christians the ideals for which the church stands, or should stand. Says Thomas Toplady in " The Cross at the Front ":

> Christian conduct must no longer be merely conventional. It must be creative. There is a call for spiritual daring and adventure. . . The church must convert Christian thought into Christian action, and teach in deeds what has already been taught in doctrine.

The church does not gain strength by tolerating religious indifference, worldliness, and ungodliness among its members in order to retain large numbers on the roll. Numbers do not constitute strength unless each one numbered contributes something to the aggregate of spiritual power. Many churches would be stronger, and better fitted for God to use, if their membership rolls had fewer names on them. Gideon's army of thirty-two thousand did not lose any strength when twenty-two thousand men who were " fearful and trembling " cowards, went home. And of the ten thousand who were left, all but three hundred were lacking in those qualities of courage, alertness, and faith, so essential to aggressive action and victory. If the nine thousand seven hundred cannot be taught and trained and inspired into men of purpose and action, men of devotion and service, the three hundred who are such men had better go on without them. " There is no restraint to Jehovah to save by many or by few " (1 Sam. 14 : 6). The few with God are mightier than a multitude without him.

Nothing is gained for the kingdom of God when for any reason pastors and churches fail to exercise a helpful spiritual watchcare over their members in order that they may become functioning members, or when the fear of man makes the church unwilling to discipline faithfully those who wilfully refuse to respond to such brotherly ministry and watchcare. A new standard for church-membership must be raised. Divine ideals of consecrated Christian living must constantly be proclaimed and something like conformity thereto be demanded of all.

When the standard-bearer of a company of soldiers advanced away ahead of the company in making an attack upon an important position, and the captain called to him, " Bring the standard back to the company," the brave soldier replied, " Bring the company up to the standard." Every unfaithful church-member is practically demanding that the standard of Christian living shall be brought back to his level. The pull of his influence is to bring the whole church down to where he himself is. Pastors and church officers and leaders should, however, earnestly endeavor to safeguard the church against this downward pull by every sort of loving prayerful effort. Christian ideals must be made real.

5. Christians that Count

We are learning that true Christian living is what counts, and that this is the great essential in Christian service. There must be no separation between these two things. Living must be service. There can be no service without life. Nothing short of the abounding fulness of the divine life filling the soul can enable any believer to render the service he ought to render. The church needs to be revitalized.

It is not money that is going to meet the world's greatest and most urgent needs though it be given in hundreds of millions. The world's needs can only be met by life. It is through giving his life that the Lord Jesus has blessed the world. We must follow in his train if we would be channels of blessing to humanity. What is needed is the actual enlistment of every redeemed man and woman in the business of the kingdom of God. " The Lord wants men who count, not merely those who are counted." The great Xerxes, when leading an army of a million men, said, " I would I had as many soldiers as men." So, as the great Captain of the hosts of God looks out upon the church, he may well say, " Would I had as many life-enlisted soldiers of the Cross as there are church-members." Why should he not have? Why should there be any camp-followers connected with the army of the Lord? Why should there be a professing Christian anywhere failing to make his life count, by the grace of God, for Christ and the salvation of men?

In a great world survey conference in Atlantic City, Dr. J. Campbell White said that in order to meet, in anything like an adequate manner, the present world's needs there must be, in the five years immediately following, an enlistment of one hundred thousand new paid workers giving themselves wholly to the service of Jesus Christ. But more than that is needed. One hundred thousand new paid workers alone could not do what needs to be done. What is needed is twenty-five or thirty million Protestant Christians unreservedly enlisted in the great on-moving business of God in the world, who will "make the entire round of life, working hours and spare moments," serve Jesus Christ for the world's evangelization and the winning of multitudes to faith in him. Every Christian should count. The larger stewardship shows the way by which Christians may qualify for this needed enlistment.

Questions for Chapter I

1. Why is a more general campaign of education in the interest of the stewardship of substance needed?

2. What is the most essential truth in the stewardship of wealth?
3. Why is stewardship living greater than stewardship giving?
4. Why is a larger and more comprehensive view of our stewardship needed?
5. What is involved in a New Testament standard of church-membership?
6. Which is easier, to become a church-member or to be a true disciple of Christ? Give reasons.
7. Is there a tendency to increase or to diminish the requirements for admission to church-membership?
8. Name some elements which contribute to church weakness.
9. What remedy would you suggest?
10. What is the greatest essential to Christian efficiency?

CHAPTER II

THE STEWARDSHIP OF PERSONALITY

1. Personality Appraised

Personality exalts man into likeness to God. It is God's highest creation. There is nothing upon which God has set a higher value, nor for which God has done so much. Personality is the most precious thing a human being possesses. It is pre-eminently of greater value than the body, as a man is of greater value than the house in which he lives, as the jewel is of greater value than the casket which contains it. The body may perish, but personality lives on forever.

We should learn to put as high an appraisement upon personality as God puts upon it. To do this we shall need to think and pray along some new lines and measure by the divine scale of values. In his "Manhood of the Master" Doctor Fosdick reminds us that the Master constantly endeavored to bring his disciples to do this. He says:

> This real self, this invisible, spiritual personality made in the image of God, intended for his character, and sure to live forever, was so infinitely valuable, in the thought of the Master, that he tried continually, by every manner of statement, to make his disciples feel with him that everything else in life must be subordinated to the interests of this supreme treasure.

Such an appraisement is essential to a true and faithful stewardship of personality. He who fails in his stewardship living at this point, he who, in other words, belittles himself and trifles with this most precious trust, will certainly fail in his stewardship in every part of it everywhere. However faithful a person may be as a steward of material things in getting, giving, and using them, he is without the real dynamic for such stewardship and misses its spiritual meaning if he has not first of all, by the grace of God, become a steward of his own personality.

The responsibility of the believer to God for what he does with his personality is overwhelmingly great. He is a steward of it in an even more solemn way than he can ever be a steward of his substance. Every man will be held accountable for what he does with himself even more than for what he does with his money, for what a man does with his money is determined by what he does with himself.   What a man does with his money only expresses what he is doing with himself.   The index is a very true one. " No man does any better with himself than he does with the money which is the stored potentiality of himself."   He who uses his money for high and holy purposes thereby uses himself for such purposes.   He who wastes his money in useless things or ways, wastes himself and seals his own moral and spiritual deterioration.   He who, Ananias-like, keeps back part of the price, pronounces the sentence of his own doom.

2. The Stewardship of Personality Involves

(1) *A Consciousness and Acknowledgment of God's Ownership*.   God from the beginning has claimed a special ownership in his people.   Of old he said to Israel:

> But now saith Jehovah that created thee, O Jacob, and he that formed thee, O Israel: Fear not, for I have redeemed thee; I have called thee by thy name, thou art mine (Isa. 43 : 1).

This is true of us.   We are God's.   He has a creation and a redemption right of ownership. " Ye are not your own, for ye are bought with a price " (1 Cor. 6 : 19, 20).   " We are the Lord's " (Rom. 14 : 8).   The price paid in purchasing us unto himself and making us his own possession is beyond all human computation.   At infinite cost human personality has been redeemed and belongs to God by that redemption right. The sincere acknowledgment of this great fact is the first step in the Christian life. Shall any man then, either saint or sinner, treat lightly and disregard the personality upon which the Lord our God has placed so high a value and which belongs to him by the most sacred claim? Shall any Christian who has come to know in his own soul something of the power and blessedness of his redemption unto God, trifle with his personality? Shall he expose himself to anything whatever that would injure or ruin it, or in any way rob God of the benefit of his own possession? Surely the owner of the vineyard has a right to the fruits of it. Surely he who owns you and me has a right to all we are and to the fullest service we can render for him. The Jews of old were charged with robbing God when they withheld their tithes and offerings, but what charge of robbery, or embezzlement, shall have to be made against those who withhold from God the most precious thing that can ever be offered to him?

The stewardship of personality involves the acknowledgment of God's ownership of us all through life. We are always his. It is this acknowledgment that places a man in right relations to both God and his fellow men in his business and daily affairs anywhere. No man or woman can possibly live an unfaithful Christian life under a clear conception and full appreciation of this great truth. In this supreme fact of

Christian knowledge and experience the Christian has a great spiritual safeguard. Remembering that he belongs to God he is restrained from taking even the first step in any wrong course into which he might be tempted to go, while at the same time he is inspired to engage in many a consecrated service to which he would not otherwise commit himself. To live daily in the consciousness of the preeminent preciousness of one's personality, and that one's personality is God's purchased possession, is to put all life on the highest possible plane. Then we shall say, " I cannot do that, for I belong to God," or we shall say, " I must do this because I belong to God." This is the most exalted, the divinest stewardship any one can practise. What churches our churches would be if their members understood this vital truth and conformed their lives to it day by day! How a real stewardship of personality would save the church from the weakness and inefficiency caused by the non-participation of its members!

(2) *Making the Most of Oneself.* The tenant on a farm is under obligation to the owner, as well as for his own benefit, to cultivate the farm to the highest degree and make it produce the most abundant harvests possible. No tenant-farmer has a right to let the farm run down in its fertility and value and go to weeds and waste. Even so the Christian is under every obligation to God to whom he belongs to make the most of

himself for Christ and his service. He should so cultivate his mind and heart that he will be "fruitful in every good work." Every believer should aim to be "a vessel unto honor, sanctified, meet for the Master's use, prepared unto *every* good work." Not many are prepared for every good work. Many are efficient in one or two things, but many more in our churches have not qualified for high-class service in anything. Christian work is not in their line because they have not diligently prepared themselves for it. Multitudes of church-members excuse themselves from Christian work by saying they do not know how to do what they are asked to do. They ought to know. No Christian has a right to remain wholly unqualified for service for Jesus Christ. The church itself should be a training-school, constantly training and fitting its members for various departments of work. Every member should have his or her specific task and then in that task be unceasingly preparing for larger and better service. Even the pastor should not be satisfied with a college and seminary preparation for his work. He should be ever learning, ever training his powers, ever seeking fuller equipment, mentally and spiritually, for the work God has given him to do. The Sunday-school superintendent, however excellent his qualifications may be for his office, should keep pace with all progress and improvements in methods of Sunday-school work. Teachers should at the outset

take a teacher-training course and then keep fitting themselves by a study of methods, by reading the best books and periodicals bearing on
their work, and by every sort of help, for the
best service.

A few years ago a young man was elected
president of a Baptist young people's society. He
at once secured a supply of books on the organization of the society and its work, carefully
studied them, and fitted himself for intelligent
leadership in the society of which he was made
president. He made the most of himself for the
office to which he was elected. It is scarcely
necessary to add that under his régime the society
made a fine record in every way.

Unfitness for work of some sort for Christ and
the consequent inactivity are inexcusable in
church-members and should not be passed over
in silence. He who says to his heavenly Father
as he calls him to work in his vineyard, " I go,
Sir! " and then does not go, is false to his Christian profession and deserving of condemnation.
When a person unites with the church he pro-
fesses to enlist in the ranks of the army of the
Lord for duty and by that act puts himself under
Jesus Christ for orders. But if he neither at-
tempts to do anything, nor makes any effort to
fit himself for some real part in the great aggressive movements of the army, and remains idle
and useless, he deserves to be classed as a de-
serter of the cause he professed to espouse. He

certainly becomes an unfaithful steward of his redeemed personality.

(3) *Surrendering Personality to Christ.* We are to be the best possible and then definitely put that best into the hands of our Lord for him to use. The thing that Paul so highly commended in the Macedonian Christians was that *" first they gave their own selves to the Lord."* The surrender of themselves preceded the surrender of their substance. It always should. " There is that withholdeth more than is meet, but it tendeth to poverty " (Prov. 11 : 24). He who withholds his personality from God, withholds unto his spiritual poverty. He who surrenders most to God, will receive most from God. Here indeed, " The liberal soul shall be made fat " (Prov. 11 : 25). He who gives freely receives abundantly. " Spiritual poverty," says John F. Goucher, " is the demonstration of spiritual indolence, of neglected opportunities, of sequestered or misused possessions, of defalcation in the exercise of stewardship."

In this surrender the Christian finds the great secret of genuine stewardship living. It is always easier to be a steward for God everywhere else when this secret is learned. Giving substance becomes a delight when self is first given to the Lord. It hurts some people to give money for the Lord's work because they have never had the high experience of definitely giving themselves wholly to the Lord Jesus Christ.

3. The Stewardship of Personality Spells Consecration

It follows from what has been written that the new stewardship living called for in this new day of unprecedented opportunity for the evangelization of the world simply spells *consecration*. To ignore or side-step this conclusion is to miss the practical and essential thing in the stewardship of personality. If the church is to do its divinely appointed work in the world, if it is to make a powerful spiritual impact upon the community that surrounds it, its members must conform to higher standards and live more Christlike lives.

4. The Stewardship of Personality an Antidote

The stewardship of personality is an antidote to the narrowness and meanness of a self-centered life. When once a man recognizes the greatness of his divinely created personality, acknowledges God's ownership of it, makes the very best of it in every way, and then gives it all back to his Lord and Master for his service, he can no longer live in the narrow circle marked by the boundary-lines of his self-life. His personality then becomes efficiently related to the great movements for the world's redemption and betterment. He can no longer be a spiritual neutral in the church's affairs, having his name on its roll, but selfishly and sinfully withholding himself and his substance from its service. Here is the cure for the paralyzing disease of non-participation with which so many church-members are afflicted. Given that phase of stewardship called for in this chapter, and every other phase of stewardship will follow.

5. Illustrations

Joseph was a faithful steward over the material affairs of Potiphar's household, and God greatly prospered him.

And Joseph found favor in his sight, and he ministered unto him; and he made him overseer over his house, and all that he had he put into his hand. And it came to pass from the time that he made him overseer in his house, and over all that he had, that Jehovah blessed the Egyptian's house for Joseph's sake; and the blessing of Jehovah was upon all that he had, in the house and in the field. And he left all that he had in Joseph's hand; and he knew not aught that was with him, save the bread which he did eat. And Joseph was comely and well-favored (Gen. 39 : 4-6).

Joseph was a faithful steward for Potiphar because he was a faithful steward of his own personality for God. He treasured and guarded his own character, that is, what he was, even more carefully than he did the affairs of his Egyptian master. He lived his life under the eye of Jehovah more than under the eye of Potiphar. Because he did he nobly and firmly withstood the wicked plottings of Potiphar's wife to ensnare him and cause his downfall. Through her wickedness he

c

was sent to prison, but he had kept himself unspotted. Nor did he ever falter in his integrity, nor in his loyalty to the principles of righteousness and truth, whether he lived his life in the prison or in the palace as governor over all Egypt. His is a fine example of stewardship living under all circumstances, and his life abounds in inspirations for all young men to be true to themselves, to be faithful in the stewardship of their own personality.

Daniel is a similar example. In the Babylonian court, in the midst of pagan practises and prejudices, he recognized the fact that he was a steward for God of his own personality and character. He never betrayed his trust. There was nothing weak or wishy-washy about Daniel. He fearlessly faced the mouths of lions in his faithfulness, and no threats or decrees of rulers could turn him from the path of duty. The church of Jesus Christ today needs a great infusion of the Daniel-spirit. Alas, that in our times it is true not only that so many are afraid to face the lions of criticism and opposition in the service of God, but that even a mouse of difficulty or danger will cause them to run from the post of duty and consecrated service. DARE TO BE A DANIEL.

Questions for Chapter II

1. Why is personality exceedingly precious?
2. How is the stewardship of personality related to every other phase of stewardship?

3. Why is the stewardship of personality a most solemn responsibility?
4. What is involved in a faithful stewardship of personality?
5. How can we best safeguard our personality from injury?
6. What would be the effect in church efficiency if church-members generally recognized their stewardship of personality?
7. How may Christians fit themselves for better service for Christ?
8. What is the cause of spiritual poverty with many Christians?
9. What were the outstanding facts in the stewardship of personality in the lives of Joseph and Daniel?
10. What kind of Christians would men be if in all the relations of life they realized and acknowledged God's claim upon their redeemed personality?

CHAPTER III

THE STEWARDSHIP OF TALENTS

1. Life Resources and Powers

We use the word " talent " in its widest sense. Not only as " a particular and uncommon aptitude for some special work or activity," but also for the cultivated ability or power, which a person may possess, to plan, direct, and do. Every one has resources and powers of some sort and degree which he can harness and bring into action in the service of God. Every one is a steward of the ability, inherent or cultivated, which he possesses.

No person is excused from service for Christ because he does not possess the gifts or aptitudes which some one else has. Our gracious Lord is not asking for talents we do not possess, but he is calling for the faithful stewardship of every talent we have. There is a place and need in the

26

manifold activities belonging to the progress of the gospel in the world for every kind of ability it is possible for the children of God to possess. No one can truthfully say, "There is nothing I can do." One man, who may have no aptitude or qualifications for missionary work in China or Africa, or to be an evangelist or pastor at home, may have a fine aptitude for business and be successful in making money. Having this ability he is under just as much obligation to devote it to the interests and advancement of the gospel in the world as another may be under obligation because of his gifts to go into the world field and preach the gospel. Alpheus Hardy, the New England philanthropist, when because of physical weakness he had to give up preparing to preach, saw that he could serve God in business with the same devotion as in preaching, and that to make money for God might be his sacred calling. So faithful was he to this high purpose that by the money he made he did a great work both at home and abroad for Christ and his kingdom among men.

The small-talent man is by no means exempt from this stewardship obligation. The servant who received only one talent in trust from his master in the parable story in Matthew 25, was condemned not because he had so little with which to work, but because he did nothing for his master with what was committed to him. He too would have received the commendation,

"Well done, good and faithful servant," if he had done the best he could with what he had. This parable story suggests also that those who have little are quite as likely to fall down in their stewardship as those who have much, and the lesson is that the man with but little talent or ability in any respect does not escape the responsibility for a right use of what he has. The rich are often severely criticized for not doing greater things for God with their riches, and the less favored often boastfully declare what great things they would do if they possessed such abundant wealth. But the insincerity of this declaration is clearly evidenced by the fact that they fail to do the best they could and should for Christ with the resources they have, either of personality, talents, or possessions. If a man is not serving God with what he has, what reason is there to expect he would serve God if he had greater resources of any kind?

Life resources and powers, either great or small, many or few, inherent or acquired, are all to be placed on a stewardship basis. We are trustees of them and are accountable to God for what we do with them.

2. Skill

Skill is defined as "the familiar knowledge of any science, art, or handicraft, with corresponding readiness and dexterity in execution or performance." Skill may be classed under the general head of talents. There are many spheres of action in which men may be skilful. One may be skilful as a carpenter, an architect, an engineer, an artist, a musician, etc. The possession and use of skill in any line opens a wide field for the application of the principles of stewardship. To bring one's skill under the rule of stewardship principles is to glorify it. When a man devotes his skill, whatever it may be, to the service of the Lord his God, he lifts it above the commonplace and makes it a channel by which God can make the man's life a great blessing in the world.

Bezalel was appointed to the high office of builder of the tabernacle in the wilderness with all its vessels and furniture because he was skilled in work of that kind.

And Jehovah spake unto Moses, saying, See I have called by name Bezalel the son of Uri the son of Hur, of the tribe of Judah: and I have filled him with the Spirit of God, in wisdom, and in understanding, and in knowledge, and in all manner of workmanship, to devise skilful works, to work in gold, and in silver, and in brass, and in cutting of stones for setting, and in carving of wood, to work in all manner of workmanship (Exod. 31 : 1-5).

God by his Spirit gave Bezalel the skill, and the wisdom and the understanding, but it was his part to use faithfully what God bestowed in the high service to which God called him. Skill is from God and should be used for God. It is just as possible for any man to devote his skill, whatever it may be, to high and holy uses as it was for

Bezalel. William Carey cobbled shoes in order that he might advance the cause of Christ among men. A Swedish immigrant landing at Ellis Island was led to Christ by an earnest missionary. She secured a humble situation as a servant, but in it honored her new-found Saviour and out of her first month's wages brought ten dollars to the missionary, saying, " I want to help some one else find the Saviour I have found."

A man may have the presence and help of the Holy Spirit in the use of his skill in any worthy work as really as another man may have his presence in preaching the gospel to a multitude of people. The objective in one case as in the other may be, and should be, the winning of men to faith in Christ and to public identification with him.

To be a steward of skill is so to relate it to God, and the things of God, that it will serve him in whatever it may be employed. It is not to be devoted to secular or material ends but to spiritual. " Ye cannot serve God and mammon." The skilled Christian musician, either with voice or instrument, has a higher mission in the world than to use his or her musical ability to amuse and entertain the world. Tuned to the music of heaven, and dedicated to the Lord Jesus Christ, such ability should be used in the appeals of sacred song to draw souls to him.

Life with the Christian is not to be divided into secular and religious. It is all to be religious.

Whatever a man's work is, it is the sphere in which he is to express his devotion to Christ. Whether he digs ditches, or decorates palaces, or sways a multitude of people by his eloquence, he is to aim purely at God's glory in what he does. " Whether therefore ye eat or drink, or whatsoever ye do, do all to the glory of God " (1 Cor. 10 : 31).

3. Mental Equipment and Business Ability

Mental equipment is both a gift and an attainment. Mental powers vary. Some have master minds, others only ordinary, or below ordinary. The man with ordinary mental ability may, by diligent study and patient, thorough training, become a man with a master mind, and if he can he should. Many a man ought to have better mental ability than he has, and he is responsible to God not simply for what he has but for what he might have. Whatever ability a man may have to think through great problems, clearly and effectively to plan great movements, efficiently to direct the activities of others, or inspire to action by his own intelligent and splendid enthusiasm, should be placed at the disposal of Jesus Christ.

Mental equipment comes through proper and diligent reading and study. The place of good literature as an important and valuable element in the development and strengthening of our talents needs a new emphasis. The present generation is altogether too careless about its reading. There is a vast amount of literature read, but there is so much of it that is damaging to the mind rather than helpful. They who read what may be called jazz literature, sow the fields of their mind full of tares and weeds, to the destruction of the good seed that may have been planted there. When the intellectual powers are fed on useless chaff, literary garbage, and deadly poison, mental and moral ruin must follow. The amount of printed trash on which so many, both old and young, spend their time, is appalling. Talents which might have been polished and improved, and made more eminently useful in the service of Christ, by lofty and inspiring literature, are rendered unfit by the vicious character of the reading. There is an abundance of stimulating, enlightening, and uplifting books of all kinds today, and wise is he who makes the fullest possible use of these books unto his better mental and spiritual equipment. We plead for a wider reading of the best books as essential to the highest living and to the successful performance of life's tasks.

The church has as high a claim upon our minds as upon our money. What a lot of churches need in order to set them on their feet and make them progressive and powerful and successful is more brains devoted to God. Churches go to pieces and perish for lack of consecrated common sense. Their members have not been good stewards of their God-given mental powers and of their business abilities. A church that was heavily in debt, on account of a new building, allowed the accumulation of interest to increase the debt year by year until the loss of its property was threatened, simply through thoughtless unbusinesslike methods in its financial efforts. The efforts made to reduce the debt were sporadic and spasmodic, rather than regular and systematic, and failed because real thinking and good business sense and ability were not put into them. When at last, under new leadership, sensible plans were adopted, prayer and thought put into the movement, and the debt attacked in a systematic way, it was steadily reduced until it was all paid. All too often debts exist and threaten to crush the church because good judgment was not exercised in creating them or afterward in dealing with them. In many instances good brain-work would have prevented the creation of a debt.

Some Christians who have displayed excellent judgment, and remarkable far-sightedness in their own business affairs, have proposed most senseless and utterly foolish things in connection with the business matters of the church. Even wrong things, which they would not tolerate for a moment in the business world, church trustees have been known to propose in the financial work of the church. There are churches which, under the direction of the finance committee, or advisory board, or trustees, have appropriated money that was given by the people for missions, to the work of the local church. A church in a Western State collected $400 for the New World Movement which, through some evil influence, was applied to the current expenses of the church and did not reach the treasuries of the missionary societies for which the people gave it. Outside of the church that action would be classed as an embezzlement of trust funds and in the eyes of the law a penitentiary offense. How any men with any business sense, or spark of honesty, in the church can be so conscienceless as to do such a thing, is utterly inexplicable. It is neither good stewardship of trust funds nor good stewardship of business ability. Such an action is nothing less than heathenish in its divorcement of ethics from religion. The world needs more religion in business, and the church needs more business in religion. Churches would be far in advance of what they are as a felt force in their communities if Christian men realized more fully their responsibility to God for the use of their mental equipment and business ability in the service of God.

4. Power to Lead

Leadership is essential to success in the operations of any institution. Business corporations pay princely salaries to men with marked administrative ability. Men of initiative and leadership, men who can put things over, are in demand everywhere. Usually the men needed to function in this way in the business world can be found.

They are greatly needed in the church. Of course, it is always expected that the pastor will be a capable leader; he must be if the church under his ministry is to advance. But he should not be the only one in the church with the ability to lead. The church owes it to itself to train men and women for effective leadership in all departments of church work, and when in the church there are those who are capable of leading, without being bossy or officious, they should be willing and faithful in their stewardship of this valuable talent. What a host of things now left unthought of, and undone, would be undertaken and carried to successful completion, if there were more church-members able and willing to lead in doing them! So few are ready to initiate important movements and lead in making them a success. Perhaps in some instances the pastor himself is to blame for not encouraging such activities on the part of the members. Perhaps he likes to engineer everything that is done and do the major part of the work himself. If he does he makes a most serious mistake. The sense of personal responsibility and active participation in the work cannot be developed among the members in that way. No church can become one hundred per cent. efficient without men and women who have some capacity for leadership and are willing to consecrate their powers to the service of God.

What an inspiration it was to the writer

during the pastorate of a growing church in a suburban town to have in the membership a group of splendid leaders, men who gave time and thought to the work and in various ways relieved the pastor of work all too often left to him. In that pastorate they carried through the building of a new Sunday-school hall at an expenditure of over $20,000 without the pastor needing to feel the burden of the task. They cared for the financial part of the enterprise in a noble, businesslike way, with the pastor being little more than a happy associate with them in the work. Happy the pastor who has such leaders among his members. Too many churches allow their pastor to be the chore-boy for a multitude of petty little things which should be done by others, and then these churches wonder why their pastors do not preach better sermons and bring to them loftier and more powerful inspirations.

We plead for more and better leadership by church-members in the various departments of Christian work, and in putting their hearts and hands to many things that should be done but are left undone. Away with the mock modesty that keeps capable men and women from inaugurating some needed work in the church and putting it through to completion, simply because they have not been specially appointed to do it. Do not let your pastor be a pack-horse to carry every burden of the church. Lead in doing a little lifting and so contribute another factor toward making your church one hundred per cent. efficient.

5. Unused Assets

In these days of keen competition wise business management will not allow capital to lie dormant and unproductive. It is wise of course to have a wide margin of assets over liabilities, but it is not good business policy to allow surplus capital to lie idle. The same sensible policy should be the rule in connection with the great business of the kingdom of God. There should be no idle unused assets. The steward is not to hide his talents in a napkin. This means that there should be no inactive church-members and it means also that there should be nothing of talent of any kind, of mental ability or spiritual power, of personal resources or powers of any sort, that should be withheld from the service of Jesus Christ. Only thus can there be a God-honoring stewardship of our ability.

There need not be, as there should not be, unused assets in the church. Dr. W. B. Hinson says, "The unused ability of the church is the exultation of hell, the surprise of heaven, the loss of man, and the grief of God." It is the unused powers and possibilities in the lives of church-members, their shamefully unfaithful stewardship of the talents with which God has endowed them, that is crippling and defeating the church in its divinely given mission in the world. Who can estimate the power for God the church would have and what supernatural achievements would make up its history if God's people would only do what they could do?

There is something for every one to do, a place for every one to fill, a service for every one to render. For, however small a person's natural talents may be, it should not be forgotten that when a person becomes a new creature in Jesus Christ, and the possessor of a new divine life through faith, there comes to him such a heightening of power, such an enduement of the Holy Spirit, and therefore such possibilities of effective service as the man was utterly incapable of in his unregenerate state. The new born-again man is a steward of these new spiritual resources and should not allow them to be unused. They have been bestowed for ministering, for work, for the benefit of all, and that believer is without excuse who does nothing for God with the gifts the Holy Spirit imparts.

Now there are diversities of gifts, but the same Spirit. And there are diversities of ministrations, and the same Lord. And there are diversities of workings, but the same God, who worketh all in all. But to each one is given the manifestation of the Spirit to profit withal (1 Cor. 12 : 4-7).

These Spirit-given forces should not be bestowed in vain. We are in the highest degree trustees of these powers and should use them to the utmost, or allow God to use them in us and through us, for the aggressive furthering of his work in the world. The apostle Paul could say:

> By the grace of God I am what I am: and his grace which was bestowed upon me was not found vain; for I labored more abundantly than they all: yet not I, but the grace of God which was with me (1 Cor. 15 : 10).

" NOT FOUND VAIN." If every church-member could say that concerning every blessing of grace bestowed upon him, that all that God gave him by the Holy Spirit was put to use in his service, what unusual undertakings, what constant labors, what mighty achievements would characterize their lives, what surprising power and progress would mark the history of the church!

Too many are like Bobby's dad and regard themselves as " honorary members." Billy was boasting to Bobby and saying, " My papa belongs to the church."

" Mine does too," answered Bobby.

" He don't either. My dad says your dad don't never come, an' even if he does he don't put nothing in the collection-box."

" Is that so? Well, your dad ain't nothin' but a common member. My dad is an honorary member. Honorary members gets to belong to everything, but they don't hafter pay for nothin'! "

It is the unused talents, the " never-come " and " never-pay " church-members, that account for the financial deficiencies, and for the unmanned departments in the organization of the church,

D

and who cause the chariot-wheels of spiritual progress to drag heavily. There needs to be a searching out of the unused assets of every kind in every church and a new enlistment and mobilization, under the principles of Christian stewardship, of every idle asset and talent until every power and resource of the church is in consecrated action.

Undeveloped talents may be classed as unused assets, for it is as great a loss to Christ and his church for a man not to increase his knowledge, and improve his ability, and so enlarge his usefulness as it is not to use the talents he already possesses. The best way for most men to improve their powers is to use to the full the powers they have. A man becomes a better testifier and exhorter in a prayer-meeting by testifying and exhorting. A teacher in the Sunday school becomes a better teacher by diligently attending to the work of teaching. Most men become better and better givers by giving and giving. We are responsible to God for what we might be and do.

6. Wasted Energy

The conservation of energy is one of the greatest problems in mechanics. To produce more power with a smaller amount of coal, to utilize all the power that is produced so that none, or at least a very small percentage, shall go to waste, are questions that have long engaged the serious attention of men of science. Much progress has been made in the conservation of energy in the realm of physical dynamics, but enough power is still going to waste to stimulate a continuance of the search for ways of harnessing it for useful purposes. A true stewardship of life resources and powers will prevent a waste of those resources and powers. Right here the church officers need to undertake a thorough investigation of the situation and find out where energy is being spent without any advantage to the work. The question needs to be asked, " What are we doing as a church that is valueless, that really contributes nothing to the progress of the Lord's work among us or through us? " Certainly, in a faithful stewardship of one's life, the individual Christian will examine himself and inquire: " Where am I wasting any talent, any grace of the Spirit, any spiritual resource with which God has endowed me? Am I wasting anything whatever that is entrusted to me as a steward for God? Do I engage in anything that lessens my interest in the things of God and in the work that God wants to have done? Do I spend my energies in worldly matters in such a way as in any way to deprive the church of their use? Is there at any point in my life a real leakage of potentiality to my own loss and unto Christ's loss and the church's? " For a Christian has no more right to waste the talents and powers with which God has entrusted him than a banker has to waste the money the depositor has entrusted to him. It is unspeakably worse to be a spiritual defaulter and waste what should be devoted to God than it is to be a defaulter of the money of another. Christ wants us really to mean business about his business.

7. Sinful Uselessness

Then shall he say also unto them on the left hand, Depart from me into the eternal fire which is prepared for the devil and his angels: for I was hungry, and ye did not give me to eat: I was thirsty, and ye gave me no drink; I was a stranger, and ye took me not in; naked, and ye clothed me not; sick, and in prison, and ye visited me not. Then shall they also answer, saying, Lord, when saw we thee hungry, or athirst, or a stranger, or naked, or sick, or in prison, and did not minister unto thee? Then shall he answer them, saying, Verily I say unto you, Inasmuch as ye did it not unto one of these least, ye did it not unto me (Matt. 25 : 41-45).

They were severely condemned because they did nothing. Their uselessness forfeited their right to the kingdom.

Jesus made answer and said, A certain man was going down from Jerusalem to Jericho; and he fell among robbers, who both stripped him and beat him, and departed, leaving him half dead. And by chance a certain priest was going down that way; and when he saw him, he passed by on the other side. And in like manner a Levite also, when he came to the place, and saw him, passed by on the other side (Luke 10 : 30-32).

These men belonged to the Do-nothing Club, the membership of which is still quite large.

The Lord Jesus sought to inspire men to live useful, serviceable lives. He was an example of what he wanted others to be. At Nazareth, in the early part of his ministry, when he read from the book of the prophet Isaiah,

The Spirit of the Lord is upon me, because he anointed me to preach good tidings to the poor: he sent me to proclaim release to the captives, and recovering of sight to the blind, to set at liberty them that are bruised, to proclaim the acceptable year of the Lord (Luke 4 : 18, 19),

he announced his entrance upon a ministry of useful, helpful service. The poor and the captives, the blind and the bruised, were to be blessed by him. How true he was to this announcement concerning his ministry and also to the declaration, " The Son of man came not to be ministered unto, but to minister, and to give his life a ransom for many." Not a day was empty of loving ministries. We are to follow him and fill our lives with useful service. We are not to bury our talents so that our lives shall accomplish nothing for the good of our fellow men.

To be a do-nothing, as the priest and the Levite were who passed by on the other side and did not lend a hand, nor speak a word of comfort to the robbed and beaten man by the roadside, is to incur the Master's intense indignation. It was not that these men did the sufferer by the road further injury by cruel blows, but because in their pride and self-righteousness, or in their indolence and indifference, they had no consciousness of responsibility and simply did nothing, that made them worthy of condemnation. It is useless inactivity that is a bane in any life characterized by it. Do-nothingism is a deadly sin.

Our Lord and Master is very patient with us and exceedingly gracious in all he requires of us. He never asks us to do the impossible, or if he does, he will empower us to do what seems impossible, but he will not excuse or pass over our indolence and uselessness. The man who did nothing with the talent committed to him was called a " wicked and slothful servant." Moffatt translates the words addressed to him, " You rascal, you idle servant." Fenton translates, " You ungrateful idler " (Matt. 25 : 26). Thus is the man branded who ignores his responsibility as a steward of his talents and of his opportunities for some worthy and privileged service. In the teaching of Jesus there is no mercy for that sort of thing. The fruitless branch is cast into the fire. The savorless salt is good for nothing but to be trodden under foot. The useless chaff is destroyed, the harmful tares are consumed, the barren fig tree that had the advantage of three years of the best cultivation, is declared to be a cumberer of the ground. Church-members who are doing nothing for Christ, whose membership in the church is utterly barren of fruitful service, ought to consider seriously how terrible is the penalty of their uselessness.

One of the worst sins of uselessness in the church is the sin of promising to render a certain service and then never doing it, or pledging a subscription to the current expenses of the church, or to missions, and then deliberately ignoring the obligation and giving nothing. Instances of this sort of unfaithfulness are not at all uncommon as every pastor knows. There are so many people who are not dependable. You expect them to do a certain thing, and they fail. They may be at the post of duty, and they may not. They may do what they promised, but you cannot be certain that they will. Every pastor knows by painful experience what a disappointment and what a burden such people are, and how difficult it is to enlist them in some task which they may be relied upon to perform.

In our day for the sake of the integrity of Christian character, the progress of the Christian church, and the salvation of the world, we need a new hatred of uselessness in institutions and persons, and a new baptism of the spirit of sacrificial and effective service.[1]

> Time worketh, let me work too,
> Time undoeth, let me do.
> Busy as time my work I ply
> Till I rest in the rest of eternity.
>
> Sin worketh, let me work too,
> Sin undoeth, let me do.
> Busy as sin my work I ply
> Till I rest in the rest of eternity.

[1] Fosdick.

Death worketh, let me work too,
Death undoeth, let me do.
Busy as death my work I ply
Till I rest in the rest of eternity.[2]

Questions for Chapter III

1. What is included in the term " talent "?
2. Why should every talent we possess be consecrated to Christ?
3. What is the difference between the stewardship of personality and the stewardship of talents?
4. Why is the failure of the small talent man as inexcusable as the failure of the large talent man?
5. How may one bring one's skill, whatever it may be, under the rule of stewardship principles?
6. Why should the Christian regard all life as religious?
7. Name the best methods for increasing one's mental equipment.
8. Name some perils to proper mental development.
9. Has any church a right to use missionary or benevolent funds to pay current expenses?
10. Which is the greater wrong, to leave excellent talents unused for Christ, or to neglect the development of those possessed?
11. How may one's talents be wasted?

[2] Bonar.

CHAPTER IV

THE STEWARDSHIP OF A CALLING

1. Choosing a Life-work

Every man should determine to do something definite with his life. Man was not made to be a piece of driftwood, floating aimlessly about through the years and being of no real benefit to himself or to others. He was intended to be a worker, to choose some worthy calling in life, fit himself for it and devote himself to it. Scarcely any more serious or critical hour ever comes to young people than the hour when they decide what their life-calling shall be. Issues for time and eternity hinge on the decisions arrived at in that hour. At no point should any one be more conscious of the solemn responsibilities of living than just then. The fact of one's stewardship in that crisis makes the responsibility. Because in his vocation he is to be a steward for God, and faithfully serve him in and by his vocation, noth-

47

ing is more important, in deciding what his life-
work shall be, than that he should hear the voice
of God and understand clearly what his will is as
to the calling he should follow. In nothing
should greater care be exercised. In connection
with no step in life should more prayer for guidance and wisdom be offered. Dr. Francis E.
Clark fittingly says:

> For a Christian every calling must be considered a sacred
> calling. If a young man does not feel that God wishes
> him to study law he has no right to be a lawyer. If a
> young woman does not feel that God wishes her to be
> a teacher of music she has no right to teach music. Like
> the consecrated cobbler who said his business was serving
> the Lord but that he mended shoes to pay expenses, young
> people must choose a life occupation because they believe
> that is the one which enables them best to serve the Lord.

" Is this the thing God wants me to do? " should
be sincerely asked as a man faces some particular
vocation, and not a step forward should he be
willing to take until as clear an affirmative answer
as possible comes to that question.

No man has a right to throw his life away. A
man's calling should never be the napkin in which
he would hide his talents, it should rather be the
instrument or opportunity by which he would
make the fullest use of his talents for God. Because a man is a steward of his redeemed personality he should guard against going through life
without a vision of some worth-while vocation in
which he could honor God and do good to his

fellow men. <u>Putting his life as to his calling on a
stewardship basis will bring him into partnership
with God in his vocation and stir his whole being
to the highest endeavor</u>.

This sense of stewardship is a great awakener of power.
There was no power in Moses while he thought of his slow
and stuttering tongue and forgot the entrusted message.
But when he thought of the entrusted message, and put
his tongue, such as it was, at God's disposition, and tried
to deliver the message of Israel's release, Moses emerged
from weakness into power, and became a force that
Pharaoh and the world could not push aside. Paul Revere,
feeling that he was charged by General Warren with a
truth that must be told for the welfare of others, made
his midnight ride and warned Concord and Lexington of
the approach of the enemy, the sense of stewardship putting bravery and energy into the rider. *All life takes on
a new significance as soon as we realize that whatever we
have is ours as a trust.*[1]

However humble a man's calling may be, it
should be regarded as sacred, and be quite as
definitely adjusted to God's redemptive work in
the world, as the calling and ministry of the
apostle Paul were.

Whatever their occupation, Christians have but one business in the world, viz., the extending of Christ's kingdom;
and merchant, mechanic, and banker are under exactly the
same obligations to be wholly consecrated to that work as
is the missionary.[2]

Christians, therefore, should conscientiously, con-
sistently, and courageously avoid any calling or

[1] James G. K. McClure.   [2] Josiah Strong.

occupation that would necessitate any compromise with wrong, or that would hinder rather than help them in their service for God. Any vocation that would keep the Christian from the services of God's house, especially on the Lord's day, however advantageous it might seem to be financially, should not have the slightest power in its appeal to him. His spiritual welfare and usefulness are of infinitely greater importance to him and to Jesus Christ his Lord than any material gain whatever, and no man can properly maintain fulness of spiritual life by cutting himself off from the worship and service of God in his house, and from fellowship with God's people, by an occupation that secularizes God's day. We must be watchful not to lose sight of spiritual ends in our life calling. We must be careful not to exchange foolishly the precious jewels of the gifts and graces of the Holy Spirit for the glittering tinsel of any material or earthly advantage.

2. Fixing the Aim

Here is the acid test. Why have you decided to devote your life to a particular trade, or profession, or business, or occupation of any kind? What is the object you have in view? What is the goal of your activities? Have you related it to the church, the spread of the gospel, the winning of souls to Christ? Remember in asking these questions the great fact of the stewardship of your calling is involved. We never get away

from that fact, and only as we are true to it will
the aim we have in our calling be all it ought
to be.

The aim one has will give character to all one
does, and in proportion as the aim is lofty and
God-honoring will it inspire perseverance and
courage and give zest to every endeavor. He
who aims only at making money in his vocation,
who sees more money for himself in the calling
he decides upon than in anything else, has set for
himself a low and groveling aim that will keep
his life in narrow earthly limits and eternally
endanger his highest spiritual interests.

They that are minded to be rich fall into a temptation
and a snare and many foolish and hurtful lusts, such as
drown men in destruction and perdition. For the love of
money is a root of all kinds of evil: which some reaching
after have been led astray from the faith, and have pierced
themselves through with many sorrows (1 Tim. 6 : 9, 10).

Making money may be made the means to a high
end, for one can go into money-making in order
definitely to devote it to the service of God, as
not a few faithful stewards for God are doing,
but the making of money should never be the
ultimate goal in one's life. It should not be the
end. It may be the means to the highest end.
As it is, all life will be sanctified. Dr. J. H.
Jowett asks these searching questions:

Have we learned that the spiritual sides of things are
always fundamental? Or are we still in materialistic

bonds? How is it with us? How is it with our dominant aims? Are we spending money for that which is not bread, and are we laboring for that which satisfieth not? When we arrive at our proposed ends do we enter a home of vital contentment and peace? *Do material things constitute our goal, or are they only a thoroughfare to the secret things of the Spirit?* Do we believe that material things are only rightly handled when they are the instruments of God's holy will? Nay, even better than this, do we believe that things are only ordered aright when they become channels of God's Spirit, and all uses are determined and pervaded by his love and grace? Have we learned that lesson?

There needs to be a spiritualizing of the purposes for which people live. Let the aim of life be spiritual and the way or method by which the goal is reached cannot be unrighteous. They who, as stewards of their calling and career, relate their lives to God, look upon their life-work as divinely appointed for them and divinely entrusted to them, and who go forward with the supreme aim to glorify God in all they do, will have the Holy Spirit as their source of wisdom and power, and will live in abiding fellowship with the Father and his Son Jesus Christ. Putting our calling and career in life upon this high level does not lessen the importance of the minor objects of life, such as the securing of the necessaries and comforts of life for ourselves and those depending on us. It will rather exalt and glorify those minor objects and link them with the eternal.

3. Partnership with God

True stewardship living and service are not possible without making our partnership with God very real to our own souls. No thoughtful Christian will deny that he depends upon God for all things in his life. All he has comes from above.

Every good gift and every perfect gift is from above, coming down from the Father of lights, with whom can be no variation, neither shadow that is cast by turning (James 1 : 17). What hast thou that thou didst not receive? (1 Cor. 4 : 7).

All his faculties and talents are divinely bestowed. If he is following the right vocation, it is because God has called him into it. When a man is a faithful steward of the calling into which God has called him, his life, in a very real way, is in partnership with God. He goes on in his life as one of God's coworkers and has a sense of certainty and peace in all he undertakes. He lives his life with God and for God. He is not alone in what he does, for He who sovereignly rules the universe is with him, leading him, giving him wisdom, strengthening him, prospering him, and making his life a success.

The apostle Paul has given a wise word of counsel concerning any calling to which the believer may devote himself. " Brethren, let each man, wherein he was called, therein abide with God " (1 Cor. 7 : 24). "THEREIN ABIDE

WITH GOD." That means to engage in one's life-work in an abiding *partnership* with God. It means to regard him as the Chief Partner. If a man's business, or vocation, is of such a character that he cannot have his heavenly Father with him in it as the Chief Partner, he ought to give it up. No man can afford to go on in any life-work without God's presence and blessing. In his calling he is to abide in *fellowship* with God, and fellowship with God is preserved so long as we act in harmony with his will. In his calling he is to abide in *dependence* upon God, not trusting in his own wisdom or ability, but by prayer and faith seeking the divine guidance and blessing in all he does. In his calling he is to abide in *cooperation* with God, being a coworker with him in the great work of redemption which he is carrying forward in the world.

Recognizing his partnership with God in his calling greatly emphasizes a man's stewardship of his calling, holds his life in a right relation to God in all his transactions, and makes his life count for most in his service. A man's life cannot fail, nor be fruitless, when it is bound up in a partnership covenant, by a surrender of consecration, with the Sovereign Possessor of heaven and earth. In that sacred relationship the impossible may be undertaken. Then the servant of God can go forth to his war, whatever it may be, crying, " The battle is the Lord's." Victory will be certain. Defeat will be impossible.

He who commits himself to the program of the

Lord Jesus Christ hears him say, " All power is
given unto me in heaven and on earth." As in his
vocation he is ever true to that program, and devotes his life to making disciples of all nations,
he has the assuring, and heartening, and inspiring promise, " Lo, I am with you always." In
the tasks of life, in the office or factory, in the
profession or trade, or in any activity in the life
of the church, it is this pledge of the Master's
all-power and presence that gives poise and peace,
confidence and courage and victory.

4. Zeal

When a man is mastered by a high conviction
of duty, is possessed by a lofty conception of his
calling, regards it as heaven-appointed, realizes
that in it he is in partnership with God, it will
be impossible for him to live and serve in a cold
and perfunctory manner. He will be moved to
enthusiastic, zealous action. He will be all
aflame with burning zeal for the Lord Jesus and
his cause. It has been said, " There is no dynamo
generating such voltage as comes from the power
of a princely passion." The Christian steward in
this twentieth century needs more of that mighty
voltage. We are powerless because we are zeal-
less. The church fails to do its full work in the
world because its members have lost their first
love, and consequently their first zeal. We have
become too fond of ease and comfort and are not
stirred by a consuming zeal to render heroic sacri-

E

ficial service for Christ and the souls of men.
We are altogether too sparing of ourselves and
all too ready to shift the responsibility for the
performance of certain duties onto some one else.
We are afraid of being called fanatics in the service of Christ by an age that has gone mad over
its follies. The world is greatly in need of a few
blazing Elijahs who will burn their testimony
for truth and righteousness in upon the con-
sciences of men as Elijah did on Mount Carmel,
a few men like John the Baptist who has been
called the Apostle of Holy Fires, of whom Jesus
said, " He was a *burning* and a shining light."
What zeal we have is too much like a flaring sky-
rocket that quickly burns itself out. We need a
zeal in our life-work that will be so constantly fed
by the oil of the grace and Spirit of God that nothing will be able to· quench it, a zeal that will continue while life shall last. The age calls for a zeal
for Christ and his work that will not burn out in a
day, but that will rather become more and more
intense and like a forest-fire will spread in every
direction until it will be beyond the control of our
dead, cold formalism and our empty conventionali-
ties. A superficial dilettante Christianity that has
neither ironlike spiritual fiber nor burning zeal for
God is about as much use to bless and save the
world as a butterfly is to quench a destructive fire
or rescue those imperiled by it.

If a man's life-work is worth doing at all it is
worth doing enthusiastically. A Christian should

have as flaming a zeal for Christ selling groceries
or plowing a farm as any evangelist in pleading
with perishing souls. If he sees and understands
the full significance of life and his stewardship of
life, he will have it. Our coldness repels. Churches
become refrigerators which drive people away
through their dead formalities and passionless per-
functoriness.

And to the angel of the church in Laodicea write: These
things saith the Amen, the faithful and true witness, the
beginning of the creation of God: I know thy works, that
thou art neither cold nor hot: I would thou wert cold or
hot. So because thou art lukewarm, and neither cold nor
hot, I will spue thee out of my mouth (Rev. 3 : 14-16).

> Dear Lord, and shall we ever live
>   At this poor dying rate—
> Our love, so faint, so cold to Thee,
>   And Thine to us so great?

> Come, Holy Spirit, heavenly dove;
>   With all thy quick'ning powers:
> Come, shed abroad a Saviour's love,
>   And that shall kindle ours.

5. Achievement

When a man makes the most and best of his
vocation, along the lines suggested above, real
achievement or success must follow. But every
achievement in life, instead of lessening one's
obligation, increases it and should stir the soul to
undertake new and greater tasks. Every goal
of success gained by the live business man is
made the starting-point for a still higher goal

involving greater enterprise, diligence, and devotion. So it should be in the service of Christ. Because we have actually accomplished something for him, we are not to congratulate ourselves and settle down self-satisfied and refuse to do anything else. And yet what hosts of church-members have been heard to say, " I've done my share, let some one else have a turn at it now." It ought to be remembered that no person does his or her share until the very utmost one can do is done and that right up to the end of one's opportunity and ability to serve.

> In the morning sow thy seed, and in the evening withhold not thy hand: for thou knowest not which shall prosper, whether this or that, or whether they both shall be alike good (Eccl. 11 : 6).

In the morning of life, or in the morning of one's life-work, it might be paraphrased, sow thy seed, and in the evening of thy life-work withhold not thy hand. The thing we have done is to be the stepping-stone to some greater achievement for Christ. The knowledge and experience gained in the past fit for greater service in the future.

Nothing is sadder or more heart-breaking to the faithful pastor than for members of the church, who were once actively engaged in the work, to cease to share in the work and actually become a dead weight to the church's progress. Next to those who have grown cold and back-slidden from activity to inactivity are those who,

with their increased experience and ability, limit
their doing and their giving to the scale of their
inexperience and their smaller ability. Their
service has not increased with their increased
ability to accomplish worth-while things, their
giving has not kept pace with the increase of
their income. They are like the deacon of a New
England church who, when a poor boy earning
fifty cents a day, resolved to give a dollar a year
to foreign missions, and twenty years later, when
he had become a wealthy man, held his giving to
foreign missions down to the dollar standard of
his boyhood. " To whomsoever much is given,
of him shall much be required " (Luke 12 : 48).
Not less, nor the same measure, but more, should
follow every increase in ability and blessing
which God bestows. " Honor the Lord with thy
substance and with the firstfruits of all thine increase " (Prov. 3 : 9) may be legitimately given
a larger application than to the increase of wealth.
"All thine increase." All the increase of knowledge, and power, and spiritual equipment, as well
as the increase in wealth, is to be made to honor
God. We are to be ever advancing to greater
and greater things in our stewardship living and
service. " Whatsoever thy hand findeth to do, do
it with thy might " (Eccl. 9 : 10).

6. Deterioration

Ye are the salt of the earth: but if the salt have lost its
savor, wherewith shall it be salted? it is thenceforth good

for nothing, but to be cast out and trodden under foot of men (Matt. 5 : 13).

As savorless salt is useless, so is the Christian who has lost that grace that makes him a blessing to his fellow men. Fit only to be cast out —excluded—says Jesus. "He could no more endure denatured personality than denatured salt." [3]

When a redeemed man, with all his glorious possibilities through the resources of God and the operation of the Holy Spirit, allows himself to degenerate into useless spiritual insipidity, he deserves this severe disapproval and condemnation of the Master. It is a commendable thing, over which multitudes rejoice, for the great nations of the world to scrap their costly war-ships and reduce their implements of war, but it is nothing less than sinful for the Christian soldier to scrap the powers by which he fights the battles of the Lord and become a good-for-nothing Christian and a church-member fit only to be cast out, excluded.

There is many a man and many a woman who ought to be in the very forefront in the work of the church, who are not because they have allowed some satanic influence to sap their spiritual interest, impair their power for service, and utterly unfit them for faithful participation in the worship and work of the church.

[3] Fosdick.

Spiritual deterioration, and consequent deterioration in living and service, comes through neglect of religious duty. The live coal dies out quickly when it is separated from other live coals. Inactivity weakens. The unused muscle becomes flabby.

Deterioration comes through complacent self-satisfaction with the attainment one has made, the service one has rendered. He who is content with what he has achieved will not only never do a greater thing but will never again do as well.

Deterioration in individuals and in churches comes through having no program of service. Individuals and churches alike decline because they keep moving around in a circle and never get anywhere. They never reach a definite goal because they never set before themselves a definite goal to reach.

Christians deteriorate through lack of watchfulness. "Watch and pray" lest your strength to carry on be turned to weakness, and you drop out of the activity in which you were once so useful. We need to be on our guard lest, like Samson, we sleep and some Delilah betray us into the hands of the Philistines. Pray to be kept faithful lest another gap in the ranks of active Christian forces will have to be filled through your dropping out. Pray to be kept from spiritual deterioration and paralysis. Pray that the Lord Jesus may never have to say of you, Like saltless salt he is good for nothing but to be cast out.

An unnumbered multitude of church-members have degenerated spiritually, and have therefore lost both the passion and the power for real achievement for Christ, through their neglect to have their church-membership transferred when they moved from one place to another. They were active in the church with which they first united, some as Sunday-school teachers, some as leaders or workers in the young people's society, others as officers or as active members of the women's circle, others in still other capacities, but when they moved, especially if they moved out West, they forgot their covenant obligation to "as soon as possible unite with some other church," gradually lost their interest in the church and its work, and at the same time lost their religion. Every denomination has suffered an enormous leakage in this way. There are communities where most of the churches would be filled to capacity, and the working force of the churches about doubled, if all those who were once active elsewhere were faithful to their obligations to Jesus Christ and doing their duty as his followers. These careless Christians trifle with the high privilege of membership in the church of Jesus Christ. They forget that church-membership is a stewardship and that they are under solemn obligation to him who has given his life for them to be faithful to all the sacred duties of that stewardship. Church-membership should not be trifled with.

Questions for Chapter IV

1. Why is the choosing of a life-work an important and serious matter?
2. What should govern the Christian in reaching a decision as to his life-calling?
3. How may one's life-calling, whatever it may be, be brought into spiritual relations?
4. What is the danger connected with money-making as a life aim?
5. How may money-making be made a sacred service?
6. What relationship with God is realized in a true stewardship of one's calling?
7. What great advantages come from living in conscious partnership with God?
8. May men act in cooperation with God in their life-work and not realize it or acknowledge it? Illustrate.
9. Why is zeal an important factor in Christian service, and how may it be quickened?
10. Why should Christians be as filled with zeal for Christ in so-called secular callings as pastors, evangelists, or missionaries should be?
11. What should be the influence of successful achievement upon our further service?
12. Show how spiritual deterioration may take place and one's usefulness in the service of Christ be destroyed.
13. How would a faithful stewardship of our life-calling safeguard us from such deterioration?

CHAPTER V

THE STEWARDSHIP OF INFLUENCE

1. The Fact

We cannot shut our lives away from men nor avoid the serious responsibility of the stewardship of our influence. We cannot go through life in isolation. As we come into contact with others, whether it be in the high roads of public position or in the quieter paths of private life, we are ever exerting an influence upon their minds. " For none of us liveth to himself " (Rom. 14 : 7). What we say or do influences those about us in their saying and doing. Our greatest convictions and our deepest faiths come from personal associations. It has been said, " It is not propositions, not definitions, not demonstrations, that give inspiration, but the *touch of life*." What we are, our character, our manner of life, touch men all along the journey, and each one we meet is

64

affected by the touch. We cannot escape this
fact of our influence. Even if a man were to
make a recluse of himself and cut himself off from
all fellowship with his fellow men, he could not
thereby free himself from the responsibility of
his influence. The fact that we are often unconscious of the influence we are exerting only mag-
nifies the seriousness of the fact. In his home,
in his business, in his church relationships and
activities, the Christian is ever unavoidably influencing those with whom he comes into asso-
ciation. It is his duty, as it is his privilege,
constantly to have an influence for good. That
is what he is in the world for as the representa-
tive of the Lord Jesus Christ. He is a steward
for Christ of his influence. To him Jesus says,
" Let your light so shine before men, that they
may see your good works, and glorify your
Father who is in heaven " (Matt. 5 : 16).

2. Our Brother's Keeper

Like Cain we may deny that we have any responsibility for the welfare of our brother, but
nevertheless the responsibility rests upon us. He
is being hurt or helped day by day by the life we
live. We may not take a club in our hand and
smite him to earth as Cain smote Abel, but what
we do may as certainly be to our brother man's
pain and loss. A vicious life anywhere is a peril
to the rest of mankind as really as a contagious
disease is. As some foul spot in India left in its

poisonous impurity may taint articles of clothing or adornment which may be worn with deadly effect in America, so a sinful life sends forth streams of deadly influence to the ruin of multitudes. We are our brother's keeper. We safeguard his soul or we endanger it. How unspeakably great is the responsibility resting upon us!

We are to live for our brother's good. We are commanded to do good unto all men, especially to those who are of the household of faith. Our influence is to be helpful, not hurtful. Every member of the church is to have a beneficial influence upon all other members. Each is to inspire the others to some loving ministry, to some good work.

Let us consider one another to provoke unto love and good works; not forsaking our own assembling together, as the custom of some is, but exhorting one another; and so much the more, as ye see the day drawing nigh (Heb. 10 : 24, 25).

Every church-member's influence is an asset or a liability to the church. If participating in the worship and work of the church, if contributing to its funds both for local expenses and for missions, if heartily cooperating in its activities for the evangelization of the people, and along with all this living a sincere and Christlike Christian life, his membership will be an asset of great value. But if he absents himself from the services of the church, does not contribute anything

toward its support or to the great world-work of
missions, and, instead of cooperating in its efforts
to reach men for Christ, is a grumbling, fault-
finding, trouble-making member, his membership
has an influence only for evil and is a damaging
liability. The professing Christian may inspire
scores to greater consecration and faithfulness in
the service of Christ, or he may, by the influence
of his indifference or criticism, throw a wet
blanket on every sincere endeavor made by the
church for the salvation of men.

Paul characterizes Christians as epistles known
and read of all men. The people do not read the
Bible, but they read us. Actions seen impress
more deeply than words spoken. What men see
has fourfold the influence upon them of what
they hear. This fact makes the stewardship of
the manner of one's living a great responsibility.
" Be careful where you step," said a boy to his
father as they climbed a dangerous mountain
path, " for I am following in your footsteps."
When Hirati San, the remarkable twice-born
Japanese of the gospel ship, the Fukuin Maru,
came to Captain Bickel one night and pleaded
with him to visit and preach the gospel to a certain man, and Captain Bickel suggested instead
that Hirati take a Bible to the man in the morning, Hirati replied: " He is not ready yet for this
Bible, but he has another. You are his Bible.
He is watching you. As you fail, Christ fails;
as you live Christ, so Christ is revealed to him."

So it is with Christians the world over. People are watching us, and if we fail, Christ fails, if we live Christ, he is revealed to them. We may not be happy over the responsibility of it and wish sometimes it were not so, but that does not change the fact that there are those who are getting their notions of Christianity, and of what it is to live a Christian life, from us.

3. Broadcasting

Influence is never static. It flies with the wings of the wind. No radio broadcasting-machine ever sent messages out over a wider area than a man does by his influence. Every man is a broadcasting radiograph even more powerful than the greatest radiograph man has ever made, for while the messages that are broadcast act only on the instruments tuned to receive them, a man's influence travels down the ages touching life after life all along the way. The influence we have upon one man does not stop with him, it gives character to his influence upon some one else and goes on and on touching life after life all down the ages. Our influence does not stop at our death. It is immortal. Says Dr. J. R. Miller:

Every good word spoken in this world, every sweet song sung, every holy thought or impulse of blessing started, shall go on and on, until the end of all things. In this sense our works shall follow us. The things we do for Christ here, the inspirations we put into immortal lives, the lessons we teach, the influence of good we start, shall not die with us.

This great fact emphasizes the magnitude of our stewardship of influence and makes every step and act of our lives supremely momentous. The broadcasting is going on continually. Every day adds its quota to the sum total of our influence. How prayerful and watchful this should make us.

4. A Church's Influence

Churches as well as individuals have a real influence in the world and are responsible for their influence. The apostle Paul gladly commends some churches for their beneficent influence upon other churches. To the church at Rome he wrote, " I thank my God through Jesus Christ for you all, that your faith is proclaimed throughout the world " (Rom. 1 : 8). The church at Rome was stimulating and strengthening other churches by its splendid record of faith. Located in the world's metropolis, in the midst of idolatry with all its debasing practises, and surrounded by luxury, sensuality, and vice, it required more than ordinary faith for the church to withstand these adverse influences and continue faithful in its testimony for truth and righteousness; but it stood the test and thereby manifested the constancy of its faith in God. This faith was heralded everywhere, and so a gracious influence for good went out from the church at Rome to the joy and encouragement of many others. No doubt many a struggling company of believers, whose members were persecuted because of their devotion to Jesus, were steadied and strengthened by the report that came to them about the heroic confidence in God manifested by the church at Rome.

The church at Corinth, by its interest and zeal in connection with the offering for the needy Jewish brethren at Jerusalem, stirred others to liberal sharing in that offering.

For I know your readiness of which I glory on your behalf to them of Macedonia, that Achaia hath been prepared for a year past; *and your zeal hath stirred up very many of them* (2 Cor. 9 : 2).

So too today there are churches whose liberal and sacrificial giving to missions has stimulated a like spirit in other churches. In their good works they have been an example to others and have had an influence for good as far as their works have been known.

Churches make a distinct impression upon the world around them by their character. A church that has a clean record, whose members live in love and harmony, that is prompt in paying its bills, that stands strongly for righteousness in the community, and openly opposes every sort of social injustice and wrong, has an influence for good that is felt far and wide. On the other hand, a church may have an influence of an entirely opposite sort. Factions and divisions may utterly neutralize its testimony. Its conformity to the world may destroy respect for Christianity in its community. It may cause men to stumble and create prejudice against the gospel instead of winning the people to it. A church came to be unfavorably regarded in a community because its pastors did not remain long with it, and because there was an impression that its members did not work in harmony and were much in strife. People would not go to its services. Members of its faith who moved into its neighborhood. would not unite with it. Instead of being a blessing, it became a cause of stumbling. Instead of drawing men to Christ by loving devotion to him and enlisting them in his service, it drove them away. How great and how serious the responsibility for its influence!

In the matter of a good name and the good influence which each church should have in the world every church-member is in measure responsible. Each member by his or her own life contributes to the character of the church and helps decide what its influence shall be.

5. The Ministry of Prayer

True prayer on behalf of others is most effective in influencing them in a right way and for their good. Prayer is a mighty spiritual force, for it lays hold of the divine power and under the Spirit of God brings that power to bear upon the lives of others. Intercessory prayer enables us

F

to encircle men with heavenly influences and
spiritual constraints and should be constantly
used in the larger stewardship of spiritual forces
to which we are called. We can reach and influence men by prayer when we may be unable to
reach them effectively in any other way. The
men who have had the mightiest influence for
the good of the world and for the salvation of
men, have been notably men of prayer. Paul's
ministry was powerful through prayer. Luther
and Knox, Wesley and Finney, Spurgeon and
Moody, Carey and Livingstone, by prayer
wrought wonders in soul-saving movements, in
opening new empires to the gospel, in establish-
ing and maintaining kingdom enterprises that
have blessed many thousands. The influence of
their service for Christ will outlast the stars, and
prayer was the chief element in the power and
permanence of their work. Eternity alone will
reveal what the prayers of these, and such like
servants of God, have wrought for the redemption of mankind and for the progress of the
church of Jesus Christ. " Pray without ceasing "
(1 Thess. 5 : 17). " The prayers of the righteous
have a powerful effect " (James 5 : 16, Moffatt's
translation).

6. Watchfulness

So unconscious are we of our influence, so effectively active is it when we are least aware of it,
that we need to be constantly on our guard lest

we utter a word, or take a step, or do anything
that will influence some one in a wrong way.
Even the doing of what may be perfectly legiti-
mate in itself for us to do is to be avoided if it
should cause some one else to stumble.

It is good not to eat flesh, nor to drink wine, nor to do
anything whereby thy brother stumbleth (Rom. 14 : 21).
Wherefore, if meat causeth my brother to stumble, I will
eat no flesh for evermore, that I cause not my brother to
stumble (1 Cor. 8ᵗ: 13).

We need to watch and pray that we enter not
into temptation ourselves, and we need to watch
and pray lest some one else should be led into
temptation through our influence. We need to
be watchful in order that we may keep ourselves
in high spiritual tone so that our influence may
always be the very best.

7. Examples

Dr. James G. K. McClure tells the story of the
influence of Arthur Cumnock at Harvard. When
he entered the college moral standards were low.
The students made light of excellence of character and lived loose, and many of them, immoral
lives. But this young man resolved to be true
to lofty principles, and for the four years faithfully kept the best to the front and made his life
count by its example and influence. It was not
an easy thing to enlist others in a like course,
but steadily he won other men to his side, and

at last Arthur Cumnock was honored as the one who had done more than any other to tone up the life of the college until purity and good held the highest place. He won because he had been a faithful steward of his influence.

" The Missionary Review of the World " tells of an American teacher who was employed in Japan on the understanding that during school hours he should not utter a word on the subject of Christianity. The engagement was faithfully kept, and he lived before his students the Christ-life,. but never spoke of it to them. Not a word was said to influence the young men committed to his care. But so beautiful was his character, so blameless his example, that forty of the students, unknown to him, met in a grove and signed a secret covenant to abandon idolatry. Twenty-five of them entered the Kioto Christian training-school, and some of them are now preaching the gospel which their teacher had unconsciously commended. It is the contagion of a pure Christian influence that brings people to Christ as much as anything. The faithful stewardship of such an influence has a value beyond all computation in the service of Jesus Christ.

Questions for Chapter V

1. What elements make influence a constantly active factor in our lives?
2. Why is our responsibility for our influence unavoidable?

3. What constitutes one's influence a liability and what makes it an asset to the church?
4. Which has the greater influence on the outside world, the sermon spoken or the sermon lived? Why?
5. What makes any one's influence far-reaching?
6. In what various ways may churches have an influence?
7. Why should we regard intercessory prayer as an influence for good?
8. Is prayer to be regarded as part of our larger stewardship? If so, why?
9. Why is watchfulness supremely necessary in our stewardship of influence?
10. Give instances of influence for good or evil that have come under your own observation.
11. Is our conscious influence greater or less than our unconscious influence?
12. What kind of lives will we live if we are faithful stewards of our influence?

CHAPTER VI

THE STEWARDSHIP OF OPPORTUNITY

1. Life Itself

Even in its narrower limitations and lower levels life itself is a great opportunity. But when a person is regenerated, made a Christian, and filled with the Holy Spirit, the opportunity of life is widened and enriched beyond any earthly measure. The richest, fullest, the only complete life the world has ever known was the life of Jesus Christ. It was not only the richest and fullest in its inherent qualities and resources, it was the richest and fullest in the blessings which flowed out of it for humanity. Our Lord's life on earth was his unparalleled and supreme opportunity to bless and save the world. He so regarded his life here. He constantly affirmed that he came not to do his own will, but the will of the Father who sent him. He said, " The Son of man came not to be ministered unto, but to minister, and to give his life a ransom for many " (Matt. 20 : 28).

The Christian possesses divine life from Jesus Christ, and because he does his life becomes a great opportunity to serve his Lord and to be a blessing to mankind. His commission is similar to Christ's. To him it is said, " As the Father hath sent me, even so send I you " (John 20 : 21). Along the path his Master trod with such consuming zeal, such enduring patience, such sacrificial devotion, the disciple must go if he would put the proper estimate upon his life and use the great opportunity which God gives him in it. " Have this mind in you which was also in Christ Jesus " (Phil. 2 : 5). Life in all its redeemed powers and possibilities is a sacred opportunity for highest service. What a new meaning attaches to life when thus looked upon and when we realize that we are responsible to God for the use we make of it as stewards! To misuse the opportunity, or neglect it, is to trifle with life itself. He who does not seize the opportunity God gives him by giving him eternal life, and by making him his child, and thereby opening many doors of useful service to him, lives his life in vain and despises the most sacred of all obligations. Paul said, " It is required in stewards that a man be found faithful." In no phase of stewardship is consecrated faithfulness needed more than in this phase of it.

Life's great opportunity is more than a passing incident or accident, it is the whole course of life. It is more than an open gateway to some high achievement found here and there along life's course. It is the sum total of every advantage and facility all along the way that together goes to make the high achievement possible. The supreme opportunity is made up of many opportunities, and just as these are laid hold of and used will the lofty goal of real success be reached. How exceedingly important it is therefore that every day should record the doing of what it is possible on each day to do. J. R. Miller has truly said, " We know not what momentous issues affecting all our future are involved in any quietest hour of our commonplace life." That which may seem to be of least importance may have wrapped in it some great possibility, some far-reaching issue. Because we do not know when the greatest opportunity draws near to us with all its riches of influence and ministry and power for us to appropriate, we should prayerfully fill every day with faithful service for Christ. The unknown Methodist preacher, who, in a little chapel in England, on a stormy wintry night, earnestly exhorted his hearers to look to Christ and be saved, little realized that God was giving him the greatest opportunity of his life. But that night a lad named Charles H. Spurgeon entered that chapel and heard the appeal of the preacher and obeyed it and looked to Jesus Christ for salvation, and afterward became the greatest preacher of the nineteenth century.

We make a great mistake as Christian workers

when we wait for the big event and the unusual occasion before we earnestly act and put forth our best effort. It is what may come of the opportunity, whatever it is, that makes it great. It may seem a very narrow, limited opportunity to a Sunday-school teacher to teach a small class of restless boys, but who can tell what may issue in the life of any one of those boys from the faithful use of the opportunity? It may seem sometimes to the preacher almost a waste of time and energy for him to make his very best effort when a stormy day, or some other cause, has made his congregation discouragingly small, and he may be tempted to omit the sermon or have no service at all. But who can tell how priceless the opportunity may be because of what may come of the faithful preaching of the sermon in the conversion of some soul, or in the consolation or inspiration of some saint? We all do well to magnify the great fact of our life and prayerfully regard it day by day as the supreme opportunity which God has given to us.

2. Multiplied and Magnified

This twentieth century furnishes the most and greatest opportunities for extensive and effective Christian service the church of Christ has ever had. In our day the Master is saying to his followers with a meaning and an emphasis never before possible to attach to the words, *"I have set before thee an open door."* Each generation has had its own peculiar opportunities for service, but with the advance of civilization with its increasing privileges and blessings these opportunities have multiplied in number and increased in magnitude. Every individual Christian, and every organized church, ought to be undertaking and accomplishing greater things for Christ and the good of men in these days than were ever even thought of in past generations. We are heirs of all the ages. The opportunities our forefathers had consisted largely in securing those liberties and privileges which bring to us the greater opportunities of life. As the pioneer settlers with much severe toil and suffering, and with primitive implements, cleared away the forest and gave their children the well-tilled land with fields and orchards and buildings; so those of former times have done the pioneer work in the great fields of Christian activity, both at home and abroad, at the cost of heroic toil and suffering and sacrifice, even to the laying down of their lives in many instances, and made it possible for us to occupy and sow the larger fields and reap the richer spiritual harvests. Think of the political, social, educational, industrial, and commercial privileges and advantages that are ours compared with those enjoyed a hundred or even fifty years ago. Science and invention have placed tools in our hands which enable us to speed up our activities and to do in a day what before it took weeks to accomplish. The telephone, and automobile, and tractor, and radio-graph are with us to use in the service of Jesus Christ. Our service for him ought to be speeded up and increased in proportion to these wonderful facilities. Our money offerings for the spread of the gospel have doubled in practical value in many respects in recent years. For example, a missionary on the foreign field with an automobile can cover three or four times the territory reached by the old bullock-cart method of transportation and consequently render a much greater and more efficient service. He who furnishes the automobile therefore practically puts two more missionaries in the field at the cost of one. What an opportunity!

The pioneer workers have translated the Bible into the leading languages of the world. Ours is the easier task of printing and distributing it among the nations. There is now the greatest opportunity the church has ever had to furnish millions of people with the word of God in their own language. Bible distribution ought to be multiplied in these days beyond anything ever before undertaken because the open doors for it are so many throughout the world. So on every hand the times abound with unprecedented opportunities, and we are without excuse if we do not lay hold of them and do something really worth-while in God's world work. What we do ought to exceed greatly in quality and measure anything undertaken by any previous generation.

There are many opportunities close at hand for the rendering of Christian service.

> If you cannot cross the ocean,
> And the heathen lands explore,
> You can find the heathen nearer,
> You can help them at your door.

What numbers there are in our own immediate neighborhood who have not been touched in any effective way by regenerative spiritual forces, to whom the gospel has not become the power of God unto salvation, to whom no one has brought the love and appeal of Jesus Christ!

The ends of the earth, in many millions of people, have come to America. The presence of these millions from many lands and of many tongues constitutes one of the greatest opportunities for evangelization the church has ever had. While much has been done to use this unusual opportunity, to hosts of Christians there needs to come a broadened vision concerning the foreign-speaking peoples in our land and a changed attitude toward them. Too generally race prejudice and a feeling of race superiority have " warped the humanitarian and religious conscience " and have prevented helpful Christian contacts with these alien multitudes. The opportunity to help has all too often been used for the exploitation of, and for hindering and hurting, the stranger within our gates. Antipathies must be overcome by a new baptism of love and much more made of the opportunity to be a blessing to these people. The United States will never be fully evangelized until more is done to evangelize the millions of new-comers. Every Christian should be an Americanizer and an evangelist to the aliens to the full extent of his opportunity. Because of this opportunity, we Americans have a stewardship responsibility resting upon us which can be borne by no others.

The local church does not always meet the needs of its own community in helpful ministries and in evangelizing activities. There are opportunities for real service for Christ within the reach of many churches which are entirely overlooked and neglected. The reason is because the work of the church is left so wholly in the hands of one man, the pastor. Many church-members do not recognize nor realize their personal responsibility for Christian work. Too many are slackers and do-nothings. Lay preaching has never been developed in this country as it should have been. England far surpasses us in this respect. We have done a little through organized gospel-teams, but the need and the opportunity for soul-winning efforts by this method are limitless. The distribution of tracts and good literature used to be a most fruitful method of spreading the gospel. It needs to be revived. Here is an open door that hundreds of young people and others might enter.

Every Christian is accountable to God for the

opportunity to serve. The responsibility of this stewardship rests upon every redeemed man and woman. The unfinished tasks in America among Indians, negroes, and immigrants, in the great cities and in rural districts, and the unfinished tasks in both the occupied and unoccupied mission fields of the world, furnish a challenging opportunity to the church unsurpassed by any previous opportunity it has ever had. What will the church do with it?

3. The Debt We Owe

The opportunities we have in this advanced age, because of the privileges and advantages that have come out of the lives and service of our forefathers, place us under an obligation to our own and future generations that is difficult to measure and not easy to meet. Think of what it has cost for us to have the gospel at all. For upwards of twenty centuries the gospel has been preached and passed on from one generation to another, from one country to another, from one language to another, until it has come to us in our own land and in our own language. Who can estimate what it has cost all through these centuries to preserve the gospel in the world and to pass it on and on until it reached us? The debt we owe is beyond calculation; and shall we now selfishly withhold from those of our generation the gospel blessings which others have given to us?

"I don't owe a dollar in the world," said a man complacently as a reason for not contributing to a worthy cause. "I try to live even, asking nothing and owing nothing. If other people would do the same there would be no need of so many calls for help. I don't owe a dollar in the world." "I don't believe you have one that you don't owe," promptly replied his friend. "For everything you have and everything you are that is of any value you are indebted to the past or to the present, to heaven or to earth, far more than you can ever pay. Repudiate your debt, if you like, but never tell me that in this age of safe homes, protected rights, and Christian civilization you are not a debtor both to God and to man. Why, man, you owe more than a whole lifetime of unselfish usefulness will ever repay!"

To ignore the obligation which inherited blessings and privileges have brought to us is the very height of sinful selfishness. The Christian who does nothing to pass the gospel on to others is guilty of unfaithfulness as a steward of the manifold grace of God, is robbing both God and man, and is unworthy the name Christian. To be a beneficiary of the sacrificial living and service of others, and to remain selfish, is to be an ingrate.

4. The Intakes and Outflows of Life

Our possibilities for doing good in the world, and the consequent opportunities created thereby, depend much upon the intakes of life. An empty

vessel cannot quench the thirst of the weary
traveler. An empty mind cannot impart knowledge. An empty heart, void of the blessings of
the indwelling Spirit of God, cannot convey any
spiritual good to others. We must receive before
we can give. There must be intake before there
can be outflow. God intended that our lives
should have both. We are not to be Dead Sea
Christians, all inlet and no outlet. We are rather
to be Galilee Christians with both inlet and outlet. Some Christians fail to receive; there is no
open channel from the eternal springs of spiritual
blessing and power into their souls. They cannot give out anything because they have received
nothing to give. Others fail quite as disastrously
to themselves and others because they have no
outlet through which they can be a blessing to
others.

In one of Moody's conferences a man said that
he had been living for five years on the Mount of
Transfiguration in the very sunlight of God.
"That is all very well," said Mr. Moody, "but
how many people have you led to Christ in that
time?" The man replied that he had so enjoyed
his religion that he had lost interest in the world
and its concerns, and he had not even tried to
lead any soul to Christ. And Moody said: "Man,
sit down, you are wasting the time of this meeting. A man who enjoys his religion so much
that he has no interest in saving souls has a poor
kind of religion."

The happiest and most useful Christians are those whose outflow is spontaneous and commensurate with their intake, whose giving in substance and service is proportionate to their receiving. They are channels of blessing. Having received the Holy Spirit in fulness, out from within them there flow rivers of living water. Every blessing received makes a new opportunity to pass a blessing on. Increased ability calls for larger service. As riches increase the opportunity to help spread the gospel increases. As one's contacts with people multiply and become more intimate, the opportunities to influence them in right directions, to help them to better lives and above all to point them to the Lamb of God who taketh away the sin of the world, multiply. He who socially, in the business world, or in any way, moves in a larger orbit in life, has the wider opportunity to let the light God has given him shine upon other lives to their eternal good. Using life's opportunities enlarges life's orbit.

Some neutralize the high opportunity God gives them for the best living and service by the poor stuff they allow to flow into their lives and upon which their souls feed. Right living and noble doing can never be fostered by wrong or namby-pamby superficial thinking. The funny pages of the Sunday paper furnish mighty poor mental nourishment and moral fiber for the stern duties of life on Monday morning. He who leaves the church, and its services of worship, and

G

its messages from God, out of his life, cuts himself off from the great helps to spiritual power and efficiency and cannot be a good steward of the opportunities God gives him. A life that is Godless and Christless in its intake must necessarily be Godless and Christless in its outflow.

5. Opportunities Fly

They do not stand and wait all day long for some one to employ and use them. They must be laid hold of when they come within our reach. Open doors not entered will soon be closed. Many a great cause has been lost because the opportune moment for advance and victory was not seized. The present needs and the present duties make the present opportunity and their call for immediate action. When the sun sets and the day closes all its opportunities have gone forever. No greater regret will ever come to the soul than that which will come to those who thoughtlessly and neglectfully allowed some precious opportunity, which never returned, to slip by unused. " O that I had, O that I had," day and night cried the poor crazed flagman of a train who carelessly delayed to hurry back and flag an approaching train when his own was stopped, and whose neglect resulted in a fearful wreck and great loss of life. Who can tell how great the loss for time and eternity may result from our failure to act when the need and the opportunity press upon us. *Do it now.*

Whatsoever thy hand findeth to do, do it with thy might; for there is no work, nor device, nor knowledge, nor wisdom, in the grave, whither thou goest (Eccl. 9 : 10).

So then, as we have opportunity, let us work that which is good toward all men, and especially toward them that are of the household of faith (Gal. 6 : 10).

Questions for Chapter VI

1. In what respects is life itself a great opportunity?
2. How is the opportunity for the highest service most richly enhanced?
3. Why should each day's opportunities be highly valued and used?
4. Why are there more and greater opportunities for Christian service than ever before?
5. Name some of the great opportunities for Christian work in America.
6. Give a survey of the church's unfinished tasks at home and abroad.
7. What facts increase our obligations to give the gospel to others?
8. What is the relation between the intakes and outflows of life in the stewardship of opportunity?
9. What makes the prompt use of opportunities exceedingly important?

CHAPTER VII

THE STEWARDSHIP OF TIME

1. An Entrustment

Time and life are alike given us of God to use for him as his stewards. We do not create either. They are a divine entrustment as definitely as were the talents placed in the hands of the servants in the parable. Time is so precious, and we are in such danger of being prodigal of it, that we need to pray daily.

So teach us to number our days that we may apply our hearts unto wisdom (Ps. 90 : 12). Lord, make me to know mine end, and the measure of my days, what it is (Ps. 39 : 4).

We cannot do with time as we may do with money. We cannot save it by laying it away for use in the future. Time is such a commodity, is of such a character, that if we do not administer and use it as a trust for God and his service immediately, we can never so use it. When the moment has gone it has gone forever.

Time is a sacred trust, as sacred as life itself. God has made every day of our lives precious with opportunities for speaking a kindly word, lending a helping hand, doing some noble deed, rendering some Christlike service. The moments that are so golden should be valued in the highest degree and made much of for Christ and his church. Time becomes precious to us according to the high and holy uses we make of it. The better the use we make of it the more enhanced in value does it become. Used in winning a soul to Christ, and thereby adding a star to the Saviour's crown that shall shine forever, a few moments of time have a value eternity alone can reveal. One hour's consecrated service for Christ may turn the course of the gospel into new channels of power and blessing unto the salvation of multitudes of souls. A day's doings may affect the destiny of vast empires.

The brevity and uncertainty of time, so far as we are personally concerned, give added emphasis to its preciousness and sacredness. Because our stewardship of time is limited at most to a few short years it is necessary that we be diligent and faithful in the use of each day as it comes. Not a day should pass without some definite service being rendered for Christ. When we stand before our Lord and Master to give an account of our stewardship, it will be a serious loss to us if we have allowed any of our days to pass away without anything having been done in them for him. We have thought too little of time as a sacred entrustment for which we are responsible to God.

2. The Value of Moments

An old proverb says, " Save the pennies, and the pounds will take care of themselves." The principle expressed holds true in regard to time. Value and use the minutes, and you will safeguard the hours and the days. Safeguarding them thus they will have greatly increased worth. The aggregate amount of time lost through the period of a life, simply because some profitable use has not been made of the spare moments as they come, would be startling in its magnitude if it could be fully measured. Comparatively few men have learned the art of using the spare moments of life in a beneficial way. Great watchfulness and diligent practise are necessary to success in filling up the many unoccupied spaces in life with useful activities. But he who forms the habit of making the most of his moments greatly enriches his own life and contributes most to the welfare of his fellows. Some of the greatest achievements have resulted from a faithful, well-planned use of the short periods of spare time. A busy merchant became an efficient Bible teacher by mastering a Bible Correspondence Course on the train as he traveled to and from his business.

William H. Ridgway, the interesting writer for
" The Sunday School Times," says in one of his
articles:

> Nor are these notes an eight-hour product. Every one
> is written upon a scrap of time. This particular one in
> the Atlantic City trainshed as I await the belated arrival of
> a train.

His gems of teaching and truth, which have contributed so much to the practical every-day application of the Sunday-school lessons, have been
mined and polished in those precious spare moments. So might multitudes of others gain valuable knowledge to pass on, and thereby impart
inspiration and help, by using the opportunities
the spare moments furnish. Many a man has
qualified himself for greater efficiency in business, and for greater usefulness in Christian work,
by snatching the passing moments in a study of
the best methods for the one field or the other.

" Remember that time is money," said Ben-
jamin Franklin in his " Advice to a Young
Tradesman." Just as truly it may be said, time
is knowledge and wisdom, time is opportunity
and power, time is skill and achievement. It
may be all these, and more, as it is carefully con-
served and used to advantage in these or other
realms.

Some church-members excuse themselves from
engaging in any definite Christian work in the
church by saying they haven't time. If they are

sincere in making this excuse, and their time seems to be so occupied that they cannot give any of it to the Lord's work, it is because they have not learned the secret of using the spare moments of life, or they have not planned their lives with a carefully prepared schedule of daily duties, so that they could give a portion of their time regularly to the Lord's work. One of the busiest men in the country, who is at the head of the largest business of its kind in America, and who is also on the board of directors of several great business institutions, finds time for a number of important positions in the service of his denomination and in his own local church. He seldom fails to be on hand promptly in either his business or church engagements. He does so much because his time is carefully planned. So might multitudes of others do who think they have no time for Christian work. Failure to accomplish more in life is due all too often to the haphazard use of time. A carefully prepared schedule for the day would safeguard the precious hours and secure gratifying results. Many a pastor loses out, fails to master his task and win real victories, because he dawdles away his time. A carefully prepared program, prayerfully adhered to, would save many a man from failure in his work for Christ. We need to be more faithful as stewards of time.

We can, as a rule, find time to do the things we want to do. The excuse, " Haven't time," is

often insincere because they who make it have
abundance of time for a multitude of other less
important things than the work God wants them
to do. When Christians learn to spend less time
on minor and insignificant matters and listen
more attentively to the call of God, and are
gripped more fully by the needs of humanity,
they will devote more time to the great pressing
work for the kingdom of God that needs to be
done in the world.

Far beyond words to tell is the need of willing and able
men and women who will strive with every power they
possess to serve the kingdom every day by every thought,
every word, every act of their lives.

3. Using or Misusing

There will be a full and proper stewardship of
time only as the life aims of God's servants are
high and God-honoring. The loftier the goal the
higher will be the level of the life-plan itself and
the holier will be the use made of the hours and
the days as they pass. In our stewardship of
time we must be watchful not to divorce the use
of it from the interests of the kingdom of God.
We are to honor the Lord with our time as well
as with our substance. We should conscientiously abstain from devoting our time to any
uses in which it would not be possible to glorify
God. We need very frequently to examine ourselves and sincerely ask ourselves whether we
are making such uses of the time God gives us as

he would have us make. No day should be without its record of something done in real service for Jesus Christ.

More time needs to be devoted by God's children to Bible study and prayer. We can never make the highest uses of time unless we take time to listen to what God has to say to us and to learn his will for our lives. How much we blunder, and how often we get off on some treacherous trail filled with Satan's traps, because we do not pause long enough, or frequently enough, to discover what our heavenly Father's will is concerning the way in which he would have us go. How often we do the wrong thing, or fail to do the right thing, because we hastily choose our own way and work.

There is a way which seemeth right unto a man; but the end thereof are the ways of death (Prov. 14 : 12). In all thy ways acknowledge him, and he shall direct thy paths (Prov. 3 : 6).

He who takes not time to pray cuts the line of communication with his own base of supplies and soon finds himself without the necessary materials and equipment with which to engage in battle with the enemy. He who takes time to pray makes the highest use of it, and, under the wisdom and power gained through communion with the Lord his God, will perform the task to be done not only more efficiently but in a very much shorter period. Luther used to say of his

busiest days that he had so much to do he could
not get through without two or three hours of
prayer. Ezra the priest and scribe gained both
safety and time for the eight-hundred-mile journey to Jerusalem by calling together the people
who were to go with him for a time of fasting
and prayer before they started.

Then I proclaimed a fast there, at the river Ahava, that
we might humble ourselves before our God, to seek of
him a straight way for us, and for our little ones, and
for all our substance (Ezra 8 : 21).

Individuals and churches would make more rapid
progress and accomplish greater things in their
work for Christ if they would spend more time
in prayer and supplication. There would be
fewer debts and deficits if the financial needs of
the work, both in the local church and for the
great missionary movements, were made more
definitely a matter of prayer.

There are many illustrations of the power of
prayer in meeting the problems of the church
proving that time given to prayer is time saved.
While much time may be spent in other efforts
without success, when God's people, in full dependence upon him, spread their needs before
him in united supplication, deliverance speedily
comes. A church was heavily in debt. It had a
dwelling-house property which it wanted to sell
in order to apply the proceeds on the debt. The
house was put on the market, and many people

looked at it, but no one was willing to buy. This went on for several months without any success. Then one evening in the prayer-meeting attention was called to the fact that the selling of the property had not been made a subject of definite and united prayer. It was declared that God was able quickly to dispose of the property in the interest of the work, and the people were urged to pray. Immediately the whole matter was laid before the Lord in earnest, united prayer. The answer came speedily, for within forty-eight hours the property was sold, and a substantial reduction was made to the debt that was greatly burdening the church. A church in Baltimore needed $1000 to pay off the balance due on a building site before certain funds could be secured for the new building to be erected. The pastor felt that already the people had been drained to the last penny. On the Lord's Day morning he spoke briefly on prayer, and the service was turned into a prayer-meeting in which the people prayed specifically that God would provide the needed thousand dollars. The next day a forewoman in a factory met the pastor by appointment and said to him, " Pastor, the devil has been tempting me all day not to do what I am going to do, but God is laying it on my heart to help in his work, and I want to give you this, but no one is to know who gave it." To the pastor's great surprise she handed him a $1000 bill. She then told that her father and mother had died, leaving her a few

Baltimore ground rents, and she felt she ought
to give this to the Lord for his work.

In all our church work there needs to be more
time given to prayer. We are losing ground all
along the line because prayer is given so small a
place in our lives.

> "No time to pray!"
> Oh, who so fraught with earthly care,
> As not to give to humble prayer
>   Some part of day?
>
> "No time to pray!"
> 'Mid each day's dangers, what retreat
> More needful than the mercy-seat?
>   Who need not pray?
>
> "No time to pray!"
> Must care or business' urgent call
> So press us as to take it all,
>   Each passing day.
>
> What thought more drear,
> Than that our God his face should hide,
> And say, through all life's swelling tide,
>   "No time to hear!"

The misuse and wasting of time is one of the
most prevalent of the besetting sins of professed
Christians. Wasting time in idleness or in foolish trivialities is a vice. " Satan finds some mis-
chief still for idle hands to do." If all the time
which is spent by professed followers of Jesus
Christ in petty and senseless ways were consecrated to efforts for the salvation of the lost the

world might be speedily won to Christ. A Christian man has no more right to divorce his time from the exalted world-saving service of God and devote his time and energy to mere money-making, or pleasure-seeking, than a soldier on the field of battle has to lay down his arms and give his time to chasing butterflies or to making mud-pies.

There are thousands of young men and women in America living dull and petty lives merely because devoted to petty things. There are men sitting all day on a three-legged stool who might be founding an empire. There are women "pouring tea" all winter who might be lifting hundreds of Oriental girls into new womanhood. There are able-bodied Americans without a vision, or a task, useless as chips on the stream, when they might be directing the main currents of life for a province or a nation. Devotion to a great cause makes a great life.[1]

During the war a multitude of the women of the country turned from the superficial butterfly life they were living and committed themselves with fine devotion to a thousand and one activities on behalf of the soldiers and their families. They used their refined abilities in beautiful war-work ministries, and it was hoped they would never return to spending their time in the trivial and profitless occupations of the past. Alas! how soon the reaction came after the war, how complete has been the backsliding to the old sinful waste of time! God has called his people to the

[1] President W. H. P. Faunce.

8966

most stupendous task in all the world, with issues that are eternal, and it ill becomes them to be spending their precious lifetime in that which is commonplace or useless. The Lord Jesus has a higher claim upon the time of his followers than any one else, or anything else, in all the world. His lordship over our hours and days should be fully acknowledged, and our lives should constantly witness to the faithfulness of our stewardship of time.

If a right use of time is to be made, there will need to be some new adjustments of heart and life to God and a schedule of duties must be prayerfully arranged. No man can make the best use of his time without a program to which he shall work. As we adopt God's program we have the promise of his presence in working it out, and then we cannot fail. Each of us may well ask, " How would my Lord have me use my time?"

4. Always on Duty

When a person has once enlisted under the banner of Jesus Christ as his Lord, there is no moment in his life when he is free from the obligations and duties of that enlistment. It is not as with the armies of nations in which men enlist for a limited length of time; the Christian's term of enlistment is for life. There is no discharge for him till the Great Captain calls him home. A Christian is therefore always on duty. There is no time in all his life when he can say he is excused from the service of his Lord. Having put on the uniform of a Christian profession he is not at any time to lay that uniform aside and cease to live and act as a true soldier of Jesus Christ. <u>Every hour is made sacred by this fact.</u> This does not mean that every hour must be filled with praying or preaching or teaching, but it does mean that whatever he does, whether in the common household affairs, or in business, in recreation, or in social intercourse, there is never a time when he is not a Christian and when he is not to act as a Christian. He is always under orders and he is always on duty.

No soldier on service entangleth himself in the affairs of this life; that he may please him who enrolled him as a soldier (2 Tim. 2 : 4).

Blessed is that soldier of Jesus Christ whom his Lord when he cometh shall find on duty, whatever the duty at that particular moment may be. The good soldier of Jesus Christ will live each day so that should his Great Captain come on that day he would find him obeying his orders, doing his will. A faithful stewardship of time will not fall short of this high ideal, and stewards are always required to be faithful.

There would be a more regular and constant attendance at the services of God's house, both on the Lord's Day and during the week, on the part of hosts of church-members if they remembered their enlistment for Christ and were always

{ true to the fact that they have received no leave
of absence from him. Because they are always
on duty they should be *always on duty.*

5. Procrastination

Procrastination is still the thief of time. A
slothful postponing of a service which it is one's
clear and imperative duty to perform all too often
ends in the work never being done. Procrastination, like a veritable thief, takes the opportunity
to act right away and never returns the time he
has stolen. It is gone forever. Or if, through
the grace of God and some favoring providence,
the postponed action may still be performed, it
will be without the momentum and power of the
original call and inspiration to act. A duty put
off is always harder to do when at last it may be
undertaken. A true steward of time will not
allow himself to be dominated by a procrastinat-
ing spirit. In his activities in the church he will
act promptly and will do with his might whatever
his hands find to do. He will neither waste his
own time nor rob others of its precious moments
by being late in getting to any meeting in which
he is to have a part. Unpunctuality on the part
of church-members in meeting their church engagements is, for the most part, wholly inexcusable.

A Sunday-school superintendent who is habitually several minutes late in getting to the church,
or who allows five or ten minutes to pass beyond

H

the time for opening the school before he announces the first hymn, puts the whole work of the school under a handicap and makes impossible the full success of the session. Others in the choir, or on committees, or on church boards of any kind, are unfaithful as stewards of time when they fail to be punctual in reaching appointed meetings. A young man who was five minutes late in meeting a business appointment, where a dozen men had to wait till he came, received a deserved rebuke when the chairman of the meeting told him he had robbed the busy men, who had met, of a whole hour of precious time by taking five minutes from each of them while they waited for him. Many a good cause has suffered infinite loss through careless, needless dilatoriness.

God has written the word "NOW" in large letters in the gospel message and commission. "Behold NOW is the acceptable time, behold NOW is the day of salvation" (2 Cor. 6 : 2). The apostle is writing to Christians as workers together with God and is pleading for action on the ground that God's day of salvation is NOW.

6. Giving Money but not Time

Sometimes it is harder to give money than it is to do some other things. Many women in our churches, seemingly, would rather work and fuss with church dinners and fairs than give of their substance directly into the treasury of the church.

They congratulate themselves on doing a great thing when by these indirect methods they raise a lot of money for the church. The fact is that if they would analyze their activities, and count all the cost of time and labor and materials, and put the value directly into the treasury, they would have contributed quite as much as they raised, and would have saved themselves the physical toil, and spared themselves the headaches and the heartaches, which too often result from such efforts.

But, as a rule, it is easier to give money than it is to give time to the Lord's work. Men will say, "Here is a check for one hundred dollars, but please do not put me on a committee nor ask me to give my time in any way, I am too busy." The Christian man who realizes that he is always on duty in the Lord's army and that he is God's steward of time, and is therefore under obligation to plan and administer and use the time God gives him for his glory, will not talk that way. A successful business man who was giving liberally of his substance to the business of the kingdom and had made generous provision in his will for Christian missions, gave this testimony, " I am giving more than half my time to constructive kingdom affairs, and rejoice that God has honored me by considering me worthy to be used of him in a small way." While this brother is not alone as a business man in devoting time to the affairs of the kingdom, the kingdom business suffers because so few are willing so to serve their Master.

One of the greatest needs of the church, in this day of urgent need and surpassing opportunity, is that a great host of Christian men and women shall recognize their full stewardship and consecrate a certain amount of time to activities directly related to the extension of the kingdom of God in the world. When the church-membership is mobilized in this way Christianity will advance by leaps and bounds in the world. We plead for time to be given to Christian work and that the entire church-membership be enrolled for some definite work for Christ and his church.

7. The Importance of the Present

There has probably been no period of time of the same length more momentous than the first quarter of the twentieth century. The world convulsions that have taken place have been staggering in their magnitude and in their overwhelming effects upon the nations. These awful upheavals have changed the entire outlook of history, and have created an imperative call and challenge to the church of Christ exceeding what has come to it in any previous age. The torn and weary world needs the great Physician and Saviour, the Lord Jesus Christ. He and he alone can heal the sin-sick world, quiet its passions, and meet its great and distressing need. The church's mission is to proclaim Christ and bring him to men. The present call is for immediate, universal, sacrificial action. "The King's business requires haste."

> The restless millions wait
> The Light whose dawning
> Makes all things new:
> Christ also waits,
> But men are slow and late.
> Have we done what we could?
> Have I? Have you?

The present is important as a time for greatly multiplying the efforts of the church to evangelize the world, and thereby hasten the coming of the kingdom, because if the forces of the church were fully brought under the power of the Holy Spirit, and one hundred per cent. mobilized for service, the ends of the earth could be adequately reached with the gospel message in much less than a single generation.

No Christian can live through these days without incurring great responsibility.

The present is a time to pray, to do, to give. It is a time for the utmost possible service to be rendered. It is a time to fill the hours and the days with self-sacrificing Christlike ministries. The days are passing with the swiftness of the wind. Our lifetime will soon be gone. Not a redeemed soul anywhere has enough time at his disposal to justify him in misspending any of it. We are to be faithful stewards of it all.

Stir me, oh! stir me, Lord, I care not how,
  But stir my heart in passion for the world!
Stir me to give, to go—but most to pray:
  Stir, till the blood-red banner be unfurled
O'er lands that still in deepest darkness lie,
O'er deserts where no cross is lifted high.

Stir me, oh! stir me, Lord. Thy heart was stirred
  By love's intensest fire, till thou didst give
Thine only Son, thy best beloved One,
  Even to the dreadful cross, that I might live.
Stir me to give myself so back to thee,
That thou canst give thyself again through me.

Questions for Chapter VII

1. Why is time such a precious trust from God?
2. Name some great and vital issues that may spring from the doings of a single day.
3. What practical use of the spare moments of life would you suggest?
4. Why do many church-members have no time for the Lord's work?
5. Why is the excuse " I haven't time " often unjustifiable?
6. How may we best consecrate our time to sacred uses?
7. Why is time spent in prayer a great advantage?
8. What place should prayer have in the financial work of the church?
9. Name ways in which time is wasted.
10. Why is postponed duty always harder to perform?

CHAPTER VIII

THE STEWARDSHIP OF SUBSTANCE

1. A Logical Issue

It will be apparent that when Christians see their possibilities and responsibilities in the larger stewardship, as it has been discussed in the preceding chapters, it must follow that all their substance must come under the rule of the principles of this larger stewardship. A man cannot separate his money from his life and deal with it on a different plane, or in an opposite way, from what he does with his life. If a man is a faithful steward of his personality, his talents, his calling, he must necessarily be a faithful steward of his possessions. Personality and possessions cannot be divorced. A man cannot be a true steward for God of the one and not of the other. If a man has not become a faithful steward of property or wealth it is evidence that he has not grasped the meaning of the larger stewardship in its great spiritual applications presented in this book. For the fruitage of a proper study and apprehension of the larger stewardship will naturally be a sincere and full stewardship of substance. Out of the prayerful cultivation of this larger stewardship in the life there will come an abundant harvest of glad, consecrated, sacrificial giving.

Because the stewardship of substance has been very fully discussed in many recent publications, and because the author has fully covered the ground in his book " Stewardship and Missions," it will not be necessary to do more than call attention to some fundamental truths on the subject here.

2. What is Included

The stewardship of money includes more than a recognition of God's absolute ownership of all things and the practise of tithing as a Scriptural acknowledgment of that ownership. Much literature has been published in which these two important truths have been specially discussed and emphasized while other vital and essential truths to a full and proper stewardship have been overlooked. Our stewardship of money of course begins in an acceptance of the truth, and an adjustment of our life to it, that God is absolute owner of all things. No advance can be made in a clear understanding of what stewardship means and involves until this is seen. Nor will the stewardship of substance have its practical issue in giving until at least a tenth is laid aside as the proportion which God the owner has fixed as the minimum by which his ownership is to be acknowledged.

But the stewardship of substance includes more than these two things.

1. *It includes all that is involved in the acquisition of wealth.* Our stewardship begins not in our giving but in our getting. The important thing, in some respects the *most* important thing, is for the Christian definitely to recognize the fact that he is God's steward in his calling, his business, or in whatever way he acquires wealth. All and every acquisition of money, whether as wages, salary, income from a profession, or from any business or investment, will be put on a stewardship basis. He will enter into a very real partnership with God in his money-getting and adjust his life at that point to the kingdom of God. Here is where the challenge needs to be made today. Here is where the emphasis needs to be placed. The entire stewardship campaign of education is weakened when the people are not brought face to face with their responsibility to God at this point. Here is the starting-point for a right stewardship in giving.

2. *It includes a stewardship administration of all that is acquired.* Stewardship means trusteeship, and trusteeship involves administration. A man is to acquire his income, care for it, invest it, spend it, distribute it, as a steward of it, responsible to God for what he does with it. No man

has a right to do as he pleases with the money that comes into his hand. It is God's, and he is to administer it for God. He is to honor God in the use he makes of it. " Honor the Lord with thy substance and with the firstfruits of all thine increase " (Prov. 3 : 9). This applies not only to giving but to every use we make of money. All expenditures for either the necessaries or luxuries of life are to be made in harmony with this divine requirement.

Right here, in money-using, is where a tremendous leakage is constantly going on. Millions of dollars are being used in wasteful and unnecessary ways that ought to be devoted to the service of God. The greatest failure in the stewardship of money is not in the matter of giving, it is in the matter of using. That is where God is robbed. When church-members habitually spend all the way from a dime to a dollar, or more, a night for the movie show, and do this several nights a week, and then give a nickel or a dime to the Lord on Sunday, the Lord is certainly not being given a square deal. When men get right with God in their money-getting and money-using, and are faithful in their stewardship in these two particulars, right giving is bound to follow.

3. *It includes consecration in giving.* In a proper stewardship of substance there will be cheerfulness and liberality in giving. Tithing will have a place in the giving, but it will not

have an all-inclusive place.   Tithing is a divine
requirement but it is not all of the divine requirement. He who tithes and never gets beyond
tithing to larger giving, has missed the true
teaching of the word of God on stewardship.

Tithing is a fixed proportion by which God
requires men to make a real acknowledgment of
his ownership of all things.

A man has no more right to determine the terms and
conditions of his stewardship than he has to determine the
terms and conditions of his admission into the kingdom of
heaven. This prerogative belongs to God and in his Holy
Word he has clearly set them forth.[1]

Just as the government sovereignly fixes the
percentage of the citzen's income which he must
pay as income tax, and the citizen acknowledges
the sovereignty of the government by paying the
tax, so the faithful steward acknowledges the
sovereignty of God and his absolute ownership of
all things by paying the tithe which God claims.
But tithing one's income does not meet all the
requirements of our stewardship in giving. The
tithe is the minimum. There is another rule
which says:

Every man shall give as he is able, according to the
blessing of Jehovah thy God which he hath given thee
(Deut. 16 : 17) ; upon the first day of the week let each
one of you lay by him in store, as he may prosper (1 Cor.
16 : 2).

[1] R. L. Davidson.

Tithing therefore is only the first step in giving. Tithing should only be the gateway to the splendid avenue of an enlarged and consecrated Christian giving. It usually is. That is, by the practise of tithing hundreds of faithful stewards have entered upon a life of giving that has abounded more and more in liberal offerings beyond the tenth. Many of the princeliest givers in the church began their definite advance toward the high goal they have reached by tithing their income. As the Lord prospered them, larger and still larger amounts were given back into the Lord's hands for his kingdom business. Many noble stewards have, like H. Z. Duke, of Texas, gone on from tithing, where they began, to giving, as he does, the entire income from their business.

A true stewardship of substance reaches its highest expression in sacrificial giving, a giving that catches its inspiration at the cross of Christ where infinite love gave its utmost for us. It was that love that constrained a poor woman in A. J. Gordon's church to give eight hundred dollars out of a thousand, and to live in a simple way on the balance, in order that the work of Christian missions might be advanced in the world. When the love of the cross constrains no offering will be counted too great to make for Christ.

It is the service that costs most that has the highest value. It cost the Lord Jesus beyond what we can conceive to fill his life so full of gracious ministries of power and blessing. When a poor distressed woman came in the throng behind him and touched the hem of his garment, and was immediately healed, it drew upon his resources of power, for he said: " Some one did touch me; for I perceived that power had gone forth from me " (Luke 8 : 46). From this incident we may reasonably believe that all his works of healing drew upon his power, his very life. His deep compassion which went out to the suffering and needy all about him was the pouring forth of his very soul, than which there is nothing more costly. But how unspeakably precious was that compassion to others, how rich were the blessings that accompanied its outflow! And if it cost the Lord Jesus beyond anything we can imagine to serve mankind and bless the world, what reason have we to suppose that we can ever render any worth-while service except at a real and positive cost to ourselves? That which costs us little has little value to others. To cheapen the service we render by doing only the things that are easy for us to do is to cheapen the benefit we bestow and to treat in undignified thoughtlessness the lofty and holy stewardship service for God to which we have been called. The man who boasted that he had been a church-member for years and it had not cost him a cent, was not within a thousand miles of knowing the first principle of Christian living and service, and had never been near enough to the heart of Christ to learn the first hint of what sacrificial service really means. He thought he gained by the littleness of the cost of his religion to him, but his attitude and action involved an infinite loss. He who saves his life loses it, he who gives his life saves it.

3. The Rewards

Faithfulness in God's service is always rewarded. When his will is obeyed in our stewardship the windows of heaven are opened and God pours out such a blessing that there is not room enough to receive it. God challenges men to test it. (Mal. 3 : 10.) When the Lord is honored with our substance and with the firstfruits of our increase, our barns will be filled with plenty. (Prov. 3 : 9, 10.) He who gives will be rewarded by having more to give.

The man in the parable who gained ten pounds through a faithful administration and use of the one pound committed to him, was entrusted with a larger stewardship. He was made governor over ten cities in the kingdom of his lord. The reward of faithful service is a commission to larger service and the joy that belongs to the larger sphere of usefulness and activity. This is the divine law of our stewardship. Not inactive repose but new and greater tasks, with new enduements of power for success in those tasks, is the reward that comes to those who in all faithfulness do their Master's will.

4. Conclusion

Suppose the principles and practise of the larger stewardship discussed in these chapters should be very generally incorporated in the lives of the members of our churches throughout the land, suppose this larger stewardship should be made the standard for Christian living by God's people generally, what would be the result? What would be the effect in church efficiency in all its various departments of activity and service? Would there be any lack of devoted workers for any work that needed to be done? Would there be any gaps anywhere that would need to be filled? Would there be any lack of men or means for the work of Christian missions at home or abroad? Would there be burdensome church debts and deficits anywhere, and would anything be able to hinder the triumphant onward march of the church of Jesus Christ in the world? We leave these questions with the reader and express the hope that those who read the book may be helped in some measure to live the larger stewardship life and render the larger stewardship service.

God wants our best. He in the far-off ages
Once claimed the firstling of the flock, the finest of the
    wheat;
And still he asks his own, with gentlest pleading,
To lay their highest hopes and brightest talents at his feet.
He'll not forget the feeblest service, humblest love;
He only asks that of our store, we give the best we have.

Christ gives the best.   He takes the hearts we offer
And fills them with his glorious beauty, joy and peace,
And in his service as we're growing stronger
The calls to grand achievement still increase.
The richest gifts for us, on earth or in the heaven above,
Are hid in Christ.   In Jesus we receive the best we have.

And is our best too much?   O friends, let us remember
How much our Lord poured out his soul for us,
And, in the prime of his mysterious manhood,
Gave up his precious life upon the cross.
The Lord of lords, by whom the worlds were made,
Through bitter grief and tears, gave us the best he had.

Questions for Chapter VIII

1. Why is it impossible to separate the stewardship of money from the stewardship of life?
2. What is the fundamental truth in the stewardship of substance?
3. On what Scriptures would you base the truth of God's absolute ownership of all things?
4. What are some of the essentials to a true and faithful stewardship of substance?
5. Why should there be no question as to the requirement to lay aside the tenth of one's income for God?
6. Is the full requirement of the stewardship of substance always met by tithing?
7. What is the highest and most Christlike kind of giving?